MW01173248

FOLLOWING
THE
INVISIBLE
JESUS

He is still turning
water into wine

MIKE JETTE

C3S Press

Following the Invisible Jesus: He is still turning water into wine
Published by C3S Press LLC
Rock Hill, South Carolina

ISBN: 979-8-218-44232-3

RELIGION / Christian Living / Spiritual Growth

Cover and interior design by Rachel Valliere, copyright owned by Michael J Jette

Printed in the United States of America

Sharon, thank you for believing in us and me when the odds were "a snowball's chance in Hades." Odds we will take any day! I hope I captured our adventures with Jesus and did them justice. It's been wonderful.

Contents

Seeds of Hope

One hundred percent of author proceeds from this book are donated to World Renew (worldrenew.net/vsla) to help fund Village Savings and Loan starter kits and training worldwide, and to Pathways Community Center, helping those in poverty and the homeless here in Rock Hill, South Carolina (pathwaysyc.org). Your purchase of this book will be helping to sow seeds of hope into thousands of lives because … Jesus is still turning water into wine.

Prologue

How does a reasonable person follow someone they can't see? Every chapter shares stories about how a loving God made himself known, available, and involved in our lives. Jesus helped to transform our ordinary lives into an especially wonderful way of living. By writing and publishing this book, I, along with my wife, Sharon, wanted to:

- Honor Jesus, the Good Shepherd. We are eternally grateful for this relationship and his love, mercy, and grace. He is worthy of our trust, and he is good.

- Recount with authenticity and vulnerability what happened when heaven's wisdom collided with our foolishness or when we heard his voice and dared to follow him.

- Encourage anyone who struggles with the mysteries of faith by sharing what it is like to follow someone you know but can't see or touch.

- Write the book I wish my grandparents and great-grandparents had written for us. I would love to know more about them, their lives, and their faith. This is a gift to those who come after us.

In the resurrection story in John's Gospel, Jesus shows himself to a skeptical Thomas and tells him, "Blessed are those who have not seen and yet have believed" (John 20:29). May God richly bless you and nourish your soul as you take this journey with us to follow the invisible Jesus.

1

"I Will Follow You Anywhere"

"My sheep listen to my voice; I know them, and they follow me."

JOHN 10:27

When I asked Sharon to marry me forty years ago, she had the good sense to say no. She was a single mom with a seven-year-old daughter, Kari, and she reasoned I'd be better off with someone else ... at least that's what she told me. I was crushed. Fortunately, she changed her mind and called a few weeks later and asked *me* to marry *her*. I said yes.

We were married on December 27, 1983, in an ice storm at her twin sister Karon's home in Haysville, Kansas. The next day, the three of us—Sharon, Kari, and I—drove to Milwaukee, where we would begin our new life as a family. Over the years since then, Sharon has often said, "Mike Jette, I will follow you anywhere." Of course, I figured that out when she risked it all, married me, and moved with Kari hundreds of miles away from friends and family. She "bet the farm" on a twenty-eight-year-old kid from Swormville, New York, and continues to do so, for which I am eternally grateful. No one had ever believed in me as she did. I love how she looks at me, and I hope that never changes. I know it's a look that has to be earned each day.

In the creation story, God said, "It is not good for the man to be alone. I will make a helper suitable for him … that is why a man leaves his father and mother and is united to his wife, and they become one flesh."[1] Sharon has been an incredible life partner, and we know what it means to become one flesh. We often finish each other's sentences and thoughts, and we act like we share one brain. Thirty years ago, we added Jesus to our marriage.

Jesus told his followers, "If any man will come after me, let him deny himself, and take up his cross daily, and follow me."[2] This book tells our story: Sharon, me, and Jesus. When you see an "I" or "we" in a sentence, it includes all three of us. In Ecclesiastes 4:12, the Bible says, "Though one may be overpowered, two can defend themselves. A cord of three strands is not quickly broken." Sharon would tell you that the best thing about following Mike Jette now is that he follows Jesus, and the three of us make a formidable team.

It has not been all rainbows and butterflies, but we've had a wonderful life. God is good, even though following him has sometimes felt unsafe and uncomfortable. C. S. Lewis captured this essence in his book *The Lion, the Witch and the Wardrobe*. Aslan, the lion, represents Jesus in the story. When Susan asks if Aslan, the lion, is safe for her to be around, she is told: "Who said anything about safe? 'Course he isn't safe. But he's good."[3] Sharon and I know God is good because as we follow him, we experience his goodness.

---

1 Genesis 2:18, 24
2 Luke 9:23 (KJV)
3 C. S. Lewis, *The Lion, the Witch, and the Wardrobe* (New York, NY: HarperCollins, 2002).

In John 10:27, while referring to his followers as sheep, Jesus said that the sheep knew his voice, and "they follow me." I don't always point it out in the stories told here, but I hope you perceive how we could hear his voice. You will see how we got better at listening and obeying him and, as a result, became better followers. This is not a book on theology, and I am not a theologian. Embedded within each chapter are many lessons gleaned from an ordinary life. I'm sharing personal stories about what it can look like to deny ourselves, take up our cross daily, and follow him. The stories aren't chronological, and we weren't following the Lord for the first ten years of our marriage.

In Rick Warren's book *The Purpose Driven Life*, the provocative first sentence is, "It's not about you." Warren says our purpose is far greater than our personal fulfillment, peace of mind, or happiness. It's greater than our family, career, or wildest dreams and ambitions. He says that if we want to know why we were placed on this planet, we must begin with God.[4]

If I could go back in time, I would tell the younger me, "It's not about you, Mike, but all those good things find their proper place when you do them with and for Jesus." I used to believe life was divided into the secular and the sacred. The only aspect that mattered to God was the sacred—you know, church activities. That isn't true, and it doesn't mirror the heart of God. All of life is meant to be sacred, not just church. Monday through Saturday matter as much to God as Sunday.

I would tell young me to cultivate a true and holistic biblical worldview by reading and studying the Bible and finding a community of people who also try to follow Jesus. Then, I would tell young me to read the Gospels repeatedly and watch what happens. This

---

4   Rick Warren, *The Purpose Driven Life: What on Earth Am I Here For?* (Grand Rapids, MI: Zondervan, 2013).

may sound simplistic or even silly, but it is how I fell in love with Jesus. I started late, but I now realize that Jesus was cultivating a sound foundation for my faith by compelling me to do this. He was shaping a new worldview that differed from the prevailing culture.

A holistic biblical worldview is that set of assumptions about the world and human existence revealed through scripture, creation itself, and God's Holy Spirit. It is the product of training ourselves in spiritual disciplines like prayer, acts of service, and Bible study in community with others. These were the activities that helped me learn how to hear from God, how to hear his voice, and how to follow him without needing to use my eyes to see. Dr. Ken Boa said, "The world will define you by default, but the Word of God can only define you through discipline. Even a dead fish can float downstream."[5] But how does the world define us by default?

The late Dallas Willard helped me understand how worldviews are formed: "Worldview … consists of the most general and basic assumptions about what is real and what is good—including our assumptions about who we are and what we should do. These 'general and basic assumptions' come to each of us from our surrounding culture. We pick them up from our earliest days, first from our family and later from teachers, friends, and ultimately from influential figures in the broader culture as filtered through books, films, television, and other forms of media."[6]

One final message I'd share with my younger self would be, "Don't be alarmed, Mike, but you will pass a lot of fish floating downstream. Just do what Jesus told you to do … love God and your neighbor." These are the habits we've been practicing, and

---

5 Ken Boa, "Biblical Risk Taking: Leveraging the Temporal for Eternal Gain," 2019 Kingdom Advisors Conference breakout session, February 21, 2019, Orlando, FL.

6 Dallas Willard, *The Divine Conspiracy: Rediscovering Our Hidden Life In God* (New York, NY: HarperCollins, 1998).

they have made all the difference. The requests that Jesus asked of us often required self-sacrifice and some level of risk. However, when we obeyed him, we experienced a sense of contentment and joy ... eventually. Not always right away. Whenever we said, "No," it was followed by some measure of regret. Regret but not condemnation. We learned that the God of the Bible is not in the condemnation business; he is in the redemption business. Whenever we let opportunities to follow him slip away, it leads to a sense that we missed out on something good. We were learning to build our listening muscles in times of joy or regret. Through trial and error, we got better at hearing his voice.

Anyone can say, "I will follow you anywhere." But it is much harder when the person you are following is invisible and often leads you in directions that seem counterintuitive, unsafe, and uncomfortable. If that person is Jesus, follow anyway.

FINDING OUR PLACE
IN THE STORY

1. Jesus promised that his followers would hear his voice and that they would follow him.[7] Do you think he meant that only for those alive at the time? How is it possible to hear if there is no audible sound?

2. Ecclesiastes 4:12 says a cord of three strands is not quickly broken. Why does adding Jesus as a partner in marriage make sense? What other places in our lives could we add him as a partner?

3. If you are married or in a long-term relationship, what do you see in your partner's eyes when they look at you? What can you do to keep that look or change it?

4. If asked to describe your worldview, how would you do so? Was it given to you, or did you build it? Can you identify how you developed it?

5. Where in your life and experience have you witnessed the separation of the secular and the sacred? Where have you seen it combined?

6. If you could go back in time, what one thing would you want to tell your younger self?

---

7   John 10:27

2

Young and Stupid

"You do not delight in sacrifice, or I would bring it; you do not take pleasure in burnt offerings. My sacrifice, O God, is a broken spirit; a broken and contrite heart you, God, will not despise."

PSALM 51:16–17

"The Word became flesh and made his dwelling among us. We have seen his glory, the glory of the one and only Son, who came from the Father, full of grace and truth."

JOHN 1:14

When the idea came to me to write this book, I knew I had to start with the bad stuff. If you knew everything I've done wrong in my life, you wouldn't want to be associated with me. Every good thing I've done or experienced has directly resulted from God's grace.

I have witnessed and participated in a lot of foolishness ... aka stupidity. Best-selling author Stephen Covey wrote and spoke about "emotional bank accounts"[8] (EBC). He taught us that we all have them and can make deposits or withdrawals in our interactions with others. Through our behavior, we add or subtract from

---

8 Stephen R. Covey, *The 7 Habits of Highly Effective People*, 30th Anniversary Edition (New York, NY: Simon & Schuster, 2020).

each other's EBCs. It makes sense, then, that when we have made many deposits into someone's EBC, a withdrawal will not do great harm to the relationship. However, if our account is emotionally overdrawn, a withdrawal of any size will negatively impact our relationship.

Over the years, I developed a twist on Covey's metaphor, a "young and stupid" (Y&S) account. I hypothesize that most of us are or have been young and stupid. (Some say that phrase is redundant.) Our Y&S accounts come pre-funded with a deposit called grace, or unmerited favor. People we are in a relationship with, typically family and friends, give us grace because they love us and we need it. I know this because many people have been very kind to me when I was young and stupid and making frequent withdrawals. I didn't make a lot of deposits because that would have been smart.

Bad things happen when you withdraw more than you deposit in other people's emotional bank accounts. It's easy to get over-drawn on a Y&S account. I exhausted the grace in my parents' EBCs during my high school years because I had a tough time making the academic transition from grade school. Report card seasons were brutal. Ask my brothers. My parents expected me to resemble my brothers' educational performance, but I didn't. Mom and Dad routinely said horrible things that I wish I could forget. Good or bad, words stick. The words they said didn't help, and there were no winners. It was a lose-lose.

During my twenties, I hurt a lot of people and did many dumb things. I was twenty-eight when we married, and I'm confident those who knew me well didn't believe our marriage would last. This was a reflection of my track record, not Sharon's. To test my theory, I have recently taken several informal surveys to ask those closest to me about the Las Vegas-style over-under bet on how long we'd stay married. Over-under bets are a wager on whether a statistic will be higher or lower than a quoted value. I'm guessing the statistic the bookmakers used for our marriage was closer to forty days and not forty years! I gave everyone good reason to doubt. So far, no one has had the courage to confirm or deny my assertion.

If you are one of those people I hurt, and I haven't said I'm sorry personally, know that I am genuinely sorry. I appreciate the grace you extended to me at the time. Thank you. I know I acted in many selfish and hurtful ways. I have apologized to as many of the people I hurt as I could. When you are overdrawn with others and out of grace, you become a borrower or, in my case, in relational default and become a beggar.

In his Bible teaching radio program in the 1990s, Steve Brown often said, "I'm just a beggar telling other beggars where I found bread."[9] Using the word beggar to describe someone these days is probably culturally unacceptable, but Steve uses beggar to refer to our broken spiritual condition. He was pointing others to Jesus as the ultimate solution to our poverty, and unlike yours and mine, God's grace is inexhaustible. As a spiritual beggar, Jesus rescued me from my depravity and welcomed me into his forever family. Being emotionally deficient or bankrupt isn't confined to our youth, however. We all continue to hurt and disappoint one another, unable to live up to one another's standards or even our own. The Bible helps us define the problem … it's called sin.

King David wrote Psalm 51 after being confronted by the prophet Nathan about his adultery with Bathsheba. With a deeply penitent heart, David confesses and prays for the remission of sins

---

9 Matthew Porter, "If God doesn't do it, it won't get done," Key Life (website), February 22, 2022, https://www.keylife.org/programs/key-life/if-god-doesnt -do-it-it-wont-get-done/.

he deeply deplores. He is willing to offer sacrifices but is convinced that God prefers a broken and repentant heart. Enter grace.

Approximately 1,002 years before the death and resurrection of Jesus, David knew the power of repentance and the gift of grace. He understood that God loves us because of who God is, not because of who we are. Philip Yancey put it this way: "By striving to prove how much they deserve God's love, legalists miss the whole point of the gospel, that it is a gift from God to people who don't deserve it. The solution to sin is not to impose an ever-stricter code of behavior. It is to know God." Yancey writes, "Grace means there is nothing I can do to make God love me more, and nothing I can do to make God love me less. It means that I, even I who deserve the opposite, am invited to take my place at the table in God's family."[10]

I realize I have nothing to offer Jesus but my brokenness and sin. He said, "I'll take it." In exchange, he gave me unconditional love, mercy, inexhaustible grace, and many (beggars) brothers and sisters like me. He put his Spirit in me. I won the spiritual lottery. You can, too. Amazing deal; amazing grace!

Did you ever dream about what you would do if you won the lottery? I have fantastic ideas about all the good I could do. Jesus informs the winners of this lottery how to collect. He says, "Follow me."[11] That's it. Then, watch and see the good you will do together as his followers.

I grew up thinking of God as "the great cosmic scorekeeper." He had a list, like Santa's, and recorded all the good and bad things we did. You went to heaven at the end of life if you had more good than bad on the books. Some bad stuff counted against us more than others. I was sure that when bad things happened to me, it

---

10 Philip Yancey, *What's So Amazing About Grace?* (Grand Rapids, MI: Zondervan, 2002).

11 Matthew 4:19

was because I had messed up—a kind of karma cause and effect. Fortunately, none of those things are true, but unfortunately, many people think they are true.

Perhaps you can imagine my relief to learn that God's love doesn't have to be earned. It is a gift of grace given freely through faith in Jesus Christ. The certainty of an eternal future with him creates an overwhelming sense of security, gratitude, and purpose. We know we were created for a purpose and are here on earth for a reason. Some who read this will be surprised to hear that our purpose encompasses far more than getting to heaven when we die. Our purpose doesn't die with us; it's transferred to another better reality where we continue to mine the depths of God's love and creative pleasure. We are promised a future in a new heaven and new earth.[12] And glorified bodies like his![13] Jesus chose and called each of the original twelve disciples to follow him. He still calls people; like those twelve, he has a purpose for you and me.

The stories I share in this book testify as to what it is like to follow Jesus and offer a sample of what we have done together. I have been writing a daily faith journal for thirty years, and there is much to choose from, so I picked a few of my favorites. Jesus is the focus of every story. His grace is extraordinary and abundant, and I was compelled to share these stories so others will be tempted to seek him themselves. He transforms the young and stupid into the selfless and wise. He is still turning water into wine.

---

12 Revelation 21:1–4
13 1 Corinthians 15:35–58

FINDING OUR PLACE
IN THE STORY

1. How are the balances in the emotional bank accounts (EBCs) you have with others (family, friends, classmates, or coworkers)? Are you making more deposits or more withdrawals right now? Are there people you need to call or write to say, "I'm sorry"?

2. Do you know God is not keeping score? If his love is not conditional or based on our performance, how can we inherit eternal life?

3. Some people think they have done things they cannot be forgiven for or feel unworthy of God's love and forgiveness. Is that you? If so, you are not alone. None of us is worthy. His grace is a gift.

4. Have you discovered your purpose and know why you were created? What do you see yourself doing five million years from now?

3

Boom

*"The wind blows wherever it pleases. You hear its sound,
but you cannot tell where it comes from or where it is
going. So it is with everyone born of the Spirit."*

JOHN 3:8

I n the 1990s, Henry and Richard Blackaby published a book and launched a Bible study called *Seven Realities for Experiencing God*. In them, they examine seven scriptural realities that Moses experienced in Exodus 3 that teach believers how to develop an obedient love relationship with God. This study came to us when it was still early in our quest to follow Jesus, and it had a profound influence. Having a personal relationship with God was new to me. My interpretation of my Roman Catholic upbringing was focused primarily on obeying the rules, with little or no regard for my relationship with him. That's more a reflection on me than on Catholicism.

One of the book's Seven Realities is that "God speaks by the Holy Spirit through the Bible, prayer, circumstances, and the church to reveal himself, his purposes, and his ways."[14] When he does, it is an invitation to co-labor with him in his work. These

---

14 Claude V. King, *Experiencing God: Knowing and Doing the Will of God*, 2020 edition (Nashville, TN: B&H Books, 2021).

new realities required a monumental but welcome paradigm shift for us. In my simple way of thinking, if God was going to bother to reveal himself to me personally, it made sense to write down my experiences. I began writing in a journal, and thirty years later, I'm still writing.

One of the first times I recognized God attempting to get my attention, I didn't hear an audible voice, but I discerned a difference in my thoughts. This was a time when I was floundering and searching for truth. All the beliefs and people I put my faith and trust in never seemed to live up to my hopes and expectations. I was discouraged because the problems of the country that our institutions and politicians were supposed to be solving were only getting worse. Their promises and solutions were empty and shallow. Warren Buffett is credited with saying, "It's only when the tide goes out that you learn who's been swimming naked."[15] He spoke of investing, but I've found it has broader applications. In Buffett-speak … the tide was out, and they were all swimming naked. I was desperate for something solid, something real. Something or someone worthy of my faith.

One day, while driving to an appointment a couple of hours away, I listened to a set of tapes narrated by Stephen Covey, who authored *The 7 Habits of Highly Effective People*. I was a big fan of Covey's work and enjoyed his teaching. At one point, I thought I heard Covey say, "We are not human beings on a spiritual journey. We are spiritual beings on a human journey."[16] It was a cassette

15 Warren Buffet, "You don't find out who's been swimming naked until the tide goes out," Warren Buffett Archive, 1994 annual meeting, April 25, 1994, https://buffett.cnbc.com/video/1994/04/25/buffett-you-dont-find-out-whos-been-swimming-naked-until-the-tide-goes-out.html.
16 Stephen R. Covey according to Quotable Quote, "We are not human beings on a spiritual journey. We are spiritual beings on a human journey," Goodreads.com, accessed July 25, 2024, https://www.goodreads.com/quotes/233709-we-are-not-human-beings-on-a-spiritual-journey-we.

tape, so I had to hit the rewind button not once but a dozen times to hear it repeatedly. A voice inside me clicked. My next thought was, "If it is true, this changes everything. I am more than flesh and blood."

At home, we have a gas log fireplace. When we flip the switch to turn it on, you hear a click, and then, BOOM! Combustion. That's what happened inside of me … click and boom! In one quick moment, my life took a sharp and sudden turn.

Before this moment, you could describe my spiritual life as a smoldering mess, an ember or flicker about to be extinguished. I reasoned that if Covey was right and I was a spiritual being on a human journey, I needed to understand how that worked. I had never owned a Bible, so I bought one and read it. I began to listen to Bible teachers on my car radio, making the most of a fair amount of "windshield time." I read books. I devoured it all. I learned that God had been pursuing me for years. He came after me, rescued me, and adopted me into his forever family. Reflecting on it now, I'm confident this was what Jesus meant when he told the Pharisee, Nicodemus, "No one can see the kingdom of God unless they are born again."[17] I was changed, different. I was reborn, a new creation, and belonged to a new family.

I loved what I was learning, and I was discovering a new purpose and direction for my life. Even though I had been attending church all my life, I realized my understanding of Christianity was shallow or, worse, just plain wrong. Jesus told Nicodemus, "No one can enter the kingdom of God unless they are born of water and the Spirit … 'You must be born again.'"[18] I was a newborn spiritual baby. A baby's growth and sustenance begin with milk, then solid food. We all learn to crawl first and then walk. It's the same

---

17 John 3:3
18 John 3:5–7

way with spiritual babies. I learned to feed myself and others with spiritual food through the help of numerous resources and patient mentors. It's a lifetime journey to spiritual maturity, not a one-time event or destination. And this analogy would not be complete if I didn't own up to the fact that, like every baby, I made my fair share of messes—smelly ones. My exuberance was often intolerable.

But the good news is that my appetite for God's truth was unquenchable. The fire inside me needed feeding. I was learning to follow "someone" worthy of my faith and trust: the Triune God of the Bible.

FINDING OUR PLACE
IN THE STORY

1. One of Henry and Richard Blackaby's Seven Realities is
    that "God speaks by the Holy Spirit through the Bible,
    prayer, circumstances, and the church to reveal himself,
    his purposes, and his ways."[19] How have you heard God
    speaking to you in any of these ways?

2. When God speaks, it is an invitation to co-labor with him
    in his work. Can you think of a time when you heard God
    speak and followed his instructions? What happened?
    Have you considered writing down these experiences in
    a journal?

3. What does being a spiritual being in a human experience
    mean to you?

4. Only some people can point to a specific time when they
    were born again. If you are one of those people, what
    happened?

5. God is still adding to his forever family. Do you know if
    you have been adopted? Do you want to be? Talk to him
    and then launch your spiritual antenna.

---

19 Claude V. King, *Experiencing God: Knowing and Doing the Will of God*, 2020
   edition (Nashville, TN: B&H Books, 2021).

4

Get Up!

"Then Jesus said to him, 'Get up! Pick up your mat and walk.'
At once the man was cured; he picked up his mat and walked."

JOHN 5:8–9

think born-again Catholics make pretty good Protestants. Catholics are required to go to church every Sunday … even in the summer! I noticed that average Protestant church attendance and congregational giving drop dramatically in the summer. Thank God for the born-again Catholics like me who still show up for church every Sunday. We can't stop. We also like the back row.

Another one of Henry and Richard Blackaby's Seven Realities teaches that God's invitation to join him in his work always leads you to a crisis of belief that requires faith and action. That continues to resonate with me because it certainly has been our experience.

One life-altering invitation came from him on Sunday, August 29, 1993. There would be a congregational meeting after the service at the Presbyterian church where we were members. We were "back row" Presbyterians, meaning we were members but didn't get involved in anything and tore out the back as soon as the final horn sounded. We were really good at that.

Leading up to this Sunday, in my devotion and Bible study time, I felt the Lord had burdened my heart to share a message at that meeting. I found the thought of this exhilarating. I was all in and fired up. Sunday arrived, and as the church service progressed, the fire in me began retreating into an ember. Fear was setting in, and voices of condemnation, audible only to me, were playing loudly in my head. It was unbearable, and I was deflating by the minute. My palms were sweaty, and my heart was pounding. I'm sure the beating of my heart had to be visible through my shirt. Rubbing my hands on my pants repeatedly did little to relieve the anxiety or the sweat. The meeting began when the pastor stood facing the congregation and said, "If your palms are sweaty and your heart is pounding, it probably means you are supposed to speak." No joke.

In the blink of an eye, I knew that if I didn't stand up and speak, I would regret it for the rest of my life. I also knew that if I did, my life would never be the same again. The voices inside my head telling me to sit down and shut up grew louder and more intense. God's invitation created a profound crisis of belief. One still small voice said, "Get up." I stood up.

The trajectory and velocity of my spiritual life changed that day. I can't recall much of anything I said. I'm confident I wasn't speaking in tongues, but every person who talked to me right after seemed to hear something different, which, I learned, isn't unusual. There is almost always a conversation playing in my head. I have a robust thought-life that sometimes resembles an FM radio station with the ability to hear parts of my favorite songs. I have heard others refer to this "mind music" that is hard to turn off as "earworms." In my encounters with God, I was learning to discern the origins of the different voices. In this experience, I was learning to distinguish between my voice, his voice, and the voices of those who want to hurt me. That day, God only said two words: "Get up." I was 100 percent certain it wasn't my voice because I wanted to bolt.

Months later, the Holy Spirit revealed several parallels between my life and the person's healing at the pool of Bethesda from chapter 5 of John's Gospel.[20] We were both invalids for thirty-eight years. His disability was physical; mine was spiritual. We were both helpless until Jesus found us. Jesus pursued us; we didn't pursue him. We were both afraid to be healed because our lives would be irrevocably changed, and we found excuses not to get into the "pool." We liked the back row. He told us both to "Get up." Both invalids trusted Jesus and got up. I'm so glad I did; I bet he was, too.

Someone told me recently that they imagined I always said yes to Jesus when I heard his voice. Nothing could be further from the truth. Sometimes, when I hear him asking me to pray for someone, I don't do it. I could be tired, in a foul mood, or even fearful. I passed a disabled car on the interstate the other day and was in a position to help, but I didn't stop because I didn't want to be inconvenienced. Is it always God talking to us in those situations? Probably not, but I can be honest and transparent because I feel secure in his love.

Sometimes, Jesus asks us to get up, pick up our mat, and follow him. In the story of the disabled man at the pool of Bethesda, the mat was what he laid on while waiting to get in. It was a part of his identity that reminded him who he was—an invisible nobody, a beggar, unworthy and not enough. When Jesus healed him, the mat now symbolized the miracle of his healing and transformation. Both he and the mat were changed. Jesus pursued him—an invisible nobody-beggar—and said, "You are worthy, and you are enough." Who does that? When Jesus comes to you and says, "Get up," something miraculous is about to happen that you won't want to miss. You should really … get up. You are worthy. You are enough. And he is still changing water into wine.

---

20 John 5:1–14

FINDING OUR PLACE IN THE STORY

1. The mat for the disabled man reminded him of how the world defined him … a nobody, a beggar, unworthy, and not enough. How is the world defining you? Is there an object or an event that continues to define you that you would like to have transformed?

2. Do you know you are worthy, worthwhile, and enough?

3. God's invitation to join him in his work always leads you to a crisis of belief that requires faith and action. Can you think of a time or times when you were afraid to do or say something you believed God wanted you to do or say?

4. No one follows God perfectly or hears him perfectly (other than Jesus himself). Make notes in a journal about what you learned about God when you said yes or no to him. What would you do differently?

5

Feed My Sheep

"The third time he said to him, 'Simon son of John, do you love me?' Peter was hurt because Jesus asked him the third time, 'Do you love me?' He said, "'Lord, you know all things; you know that I love you.' Jesus said, 'Feed my sheep.'"

JOHN 21:17

Do you love me? The resurrected Jesus asked Peter this simple but loaded question. Before Jesus's death, Peter had denied knowing his friend and teacher three times … as predicted. Fear overtook Peter's courage then, but now Jesus gently reinstated Peter and recommissioned him over a breakfast of fish and bread. Jesus comes to us at unexpected times and in unexpected ways.

I had an unexpected and astonishing encounter with the Spirit of Jesus in a hotel room in Dallas, Texas, during the early morning of August 24, 1996. It is stunning in a way that makes me say, "Man, I didn't see that coming." We were in Dallas to attend a family wedding. In the middle of the night, I was singing before God in what I can only describe as a trance or vision—singing his praise and greatness with all my heart and soul. Biblical wisdom poured into my mind like water from a hose. Love was washing over me, but there are no earthly words to describe the feeling, and I don't possess the heavenly vocabulary required to capture it, either. It was a depth of love and acceptance I had never experienced before and have never felt since. I know it was divine love, so pure, complete, and perfect, and I wanted to remain there but also flee from it, for the purity of the love would consume me. It was so exhilarating and overwhelming at the same time ... I begged God to stop because it seemed I could disintegrate if he didn't. When the intensity subsided, and as I lay there, I asked him what to do with what happened to me. The thought came, "Feed my sheep." I didn't realize it right away, but I was being commissioned in a way that was reminiscent of the call on Peter's life.

Many years after this, I read the autobiography of Charles Finney. He was an American Presbyterian minister and leader in the Second Great Awakening in the United States in the 1800s. Finney tells a story of what he called a mighty baptism of the Holy Ghost. I couldn't believe what I was reading because he described what happened to me in Dallas. He wrote, "I could feel the impression, like a wave of electricity, going through and through me. Indeed it seemed to come in waves and waves of liquid love, for I could not express it in any other way. It seemed like the very breath of God. I can distinctly remember that it seemed to fan me, like immense wings. No words can express the wonderful love that was shed abroad in my heart. I wept aloud with joy and love. I literally bellowed out the unutterable gushings of my heart. These waves came over me, and over me, and over me, one after the other, until I cried out, 'I shall die if these waves continue to pass over me.' I said, 'Lord, I cannot bear any more;' yet I had no fear of death."[21]

Waves and waves of liquid love. Yes! Finney's description mirrored my own. Knowing others had been blessed with the same

---

21 Charles G. Finney, *The Autobiography of Charles G. Finney: The Life Story of America's Greatest Evangelist—In His Own Words* (Minneapolis, MN: Bethany House Publishers, 2006).

visitation was a confirmation and comfort. Deuteronomy 4:24 says that God is a consuming fire. The people of Israel were afraid to approach him and sent Moses to go in their place. I knew from the Bible that his holiness was like a consuming fire, but Charles Finney and I also saw this characteristic in the intensity of his love.

"Feed my sheep." These three words would become, for me, the plumb line for discerning future invitations for work and ministry. How does any activity or invite fit into the call from the Lord to feed his sheep? When it lines up, I try to say yes; when it doesn't, I feel free to say no. Sharing these stories in book form suited the call when I was praying about and contemplating writing it. I believe God will use this to feed and encourage others, and I hope you, dear reader, are in that number.

In that hotel room, Jesus revealed only the tip of the iceberg of the depth and breadth of his love—and that was more than anyone could bear. When we think of that love, it makes us yearn and long for him. We are filled with anticipation for what is next after this temporal life and for our new imperishable bodies, which will be equipped to receive that love. There is no doubt that we are eternal, spiritual beings on a human journey.

Jesus continues to call and commission his followers. As was written by Rick Warren, it's never about us.[22] Those who have been "baptized by the Holy Ghost," as Charles Finney described it, were blessed to be a blessing to others. Revelations from God are imbued with divine responsibility and are pregnant with purpose.

---

22 Rick Warren, *The Purpose Driven Life: What on Earth Am I Here For?* (Grand Rapids, MI: Zondervan, 2013).

FINDING OUR PLACE
IN THE STORY

1. After hearing this story, does hearing someone say
    "God loves you" mean anything different to you? If yes,
    please explain.

2. Jesus comes to us at expected times and in unexpected
    ways. Charles Finney described his experience as a
    mighty baptism of the Holy Ghost, with waves of liquid
    love.[23] Do you think the Holy Spirit was showing off, or is
    there a greater purpose in an experience like this? What
    might that be?

3. In the post-resurrection story from John 21, Jesus asked
    Peter if he loved him three times and commissioned him
    to feed his sheep. What strikes you about those events?

4. Revelations from God are imbued with divine
    responsibility and are pregnant with purpose. What has
    God revealed to you? In what ways can you imagine he
    wants to use you to help and bless others?

---

23 Charles G. Finney, *The Autobiography of Charles G. Finney: The Life Story of America's Greatest Evangelist—In His Own Words* (Minneapolis, MN: Bethany House Publishers, 2006).

6

Blind Courage

"For we walk by faith, not by sight."

2 Corinthians 5:7 (NKJV)

Sharon and I consider moving to be an adventure. As an adventurous couple, we have moved our household many times. We've been accused of moving as soon as the windows need washing. I'm not sure what the current tally is. Perhaps we've moved more than ten times but less than twenty? I just looked, and the windows need cleaning again. Oh my.

Once, in 1993, we looked at each other and knew. You could feel a new adventure wind blowing. It started by visiting new construction model homes—a big mistake. Nothing robs you of contentment like visiting model homes or watching home makeover television programs. They should come with a warning label. We had the newer, bigger, better home virus. Bad.

It was time to upgrade our lifestyle. There was no shortage of people who encouraged us, reminding us how much we deserved this. Not one person counseled us against it. We shopped around and decided to build a new home in a desirable golf course community in Charlotte. We were thrilled to have our first beautiful dream home and took great pride in our decision to more than double the size of our tax deduction (mortgage). At the time, we had more income than we knew what to do with. Very little savings, but lots of income. Now, we had a massive mortgage and nothing left over to furnish our new space. What could go wrong?

On May 10, 1994, shortly after moving into our "dream home," we attended a talk given at our church. After a delicious church supper, we were treated to an unforgettable story by Bill Irwin. In 1990, when he was fifty, Bill completed the hike from Georgia to Maine on the Appalachian Trail with his guide dog, Orient, and without a map, GPS, or compass. Alone. Blind. Hiking the Trail was a pilgrimage to share God's love with those they met along the way.[24] He did it because God asked him to. God's invitation to a blind man to walk the entire Appalachian Trail alone is the perfect picture of the Blackabys' crisis of belief requiring faith and action. Of course, he wouldn't be alone; he would follow the invisible Jesus.

In his talk, he shared the first lesson every "thru-hiker" learns around the third day on the trail: your pack weighs too much, and you must lighten the load to complete the journey. Thru-hikers are those who plan on walking the entire 2,175 miles. Bill explained that he was convinced he only carried the bare necessities when loading his pack. This is a common refrain. He had to ditch a third of the "necessities" in his pack. Bill and Orient's story was riveting as he contrasted their hiking experience with the journey we are all taking through life.

Bill challenged everyone to consider whether we needed to lighten the load in our lives. Is the cost of your lifestyle weighing you down? Is it distracting you from more important things? How much debt are you carrying? (Debt is heavy, isn't it?) Do you have a lot of things, or do your things have you? There were many lessons

---

24 Bill Irwin and David McCasland, *Blind Courage* (Waco, TX: Wrs Pub, 1995).

to be unpacked from Bill's experience, but realizing the weight of our debt and lifestyle pierced our hearts.

Through Bill's story, we sensed God asking us to reconsider our home purchase and lifestyle. It had never occurred to us to ask or include him in the decision. We prayed before buying the house, but the prayer was, "Lord, here is what we are going to do, so please bless it." After realizing where we had missed the mark, we put our dream home on the market to sell. Undoubtedly, the Lord would be pleased with our change of heart and direction. We were going to move again. Another grand adventure! Little did we know just how prophetic that would turn out to be, but it wasn't the adventure we had in mind. The house didn't sell. The home wouldn't sell.

Soon, our "dream home" turned into a "home nightmare." The tribulation began one morning as we were getting ready in the master bath. A torrential rain outside found its way inside as gallons of water poured in through the ceiling light fixtures like an open faucet. Shocking in more ways than one. This unfortunate event was our initiation into what was to be a long, painful learning opportunity.

The Bible says in Isaiah 55 that God's ways are not our ways. This was not how we would have written this story. Our bathroom waterfall was soon followed by other misfortunes, which tried our patience and emptied our savings. The beautiful slate front porch sank and had to be repaired—twice. The wood frames around our many lovely windows rotted from water damage. Those same windows were double-paned, which helps with energy efficiency unless the seals break, which they did, and every window had to be replaced. Turns out it is hard to see through permanent fog. The air conditioner had to be replaced because it was too small for the job. The stucco in the front of the house cracked from one end to the other. We repaired the stucco and repainted the entire house. And because of where we lived, we had to replace the pitiful landscaping. And those issues weren't even the worst news.

When we were having the repairs done on the home, the house was not on the market. At one point, Sharon quit her job to be available to help with a family crisis. It was a tremendously difficult time for our family, and it was a significant income hit, but family is more important than money. We returned the home to the market, but it still didn't sell.

Soon, another financial setback hit us. We were informed that my good-paying job was being eliminated. The job opportunities were as scarce as home buyers, but I eventually landed a job. The new work, however, came with a considerable reduction in salary. And all this time, the house continued to languish on the market. To say we were discouraged would be an understatement. Many days, I made journal entries that sounded like King David ... "How long, Lord? Will you forget me forever? How long will you hide your face from me?" (Psalm 13:1).

On October 24, 1995, I wrote in my journal, "About a year ago, we realized that our home was taking up an increasing amount of our time and money. As the Lord began changing our hearts, this has become a real burden and source of sorrow and discomfort. Our home has been on the market for one month—but the Lord has not yet brought a buyer. ... Perhaps it will not be long now!" Wrong! I'm glad we didn't know it then because we were only in the early innings.

In the fall of 1997, three-plus years into this fiasco, we hired a different real estate agent. The first thing she did was measure our home, suspicious that the house wasn't as big as we thought. After measuring, she informed us that our previous listings claimed 300 square feet more than existed, equivalent to one whole room. The agent who represented us when we bought the house never bothered to measure it or question the builder's assertion. No agent who toured the home with a prospective buyer ever challenged the numbers. We didn't, either. We re-listed the house with the correct square footage and lowered the price.

Assumption and Presumption

The road to this experience was paved with assumption and presumption. We assumed it was our life and our money. It wasn't. We now know who the owner is. The scriptures reveal that God is the owner, controller, ruler, and distributor of everything in the heavens and the earth. We aren't owners; we are temporary managers, so you never see a U-Haul trailer attached to a hearse.

What we did would be the same as a UPS delivery person keeping packages. When the owner of a parcel prepares it for shipping, the expectation is that it will reach its destination. The truck driver does not regard the package as personal property. They do not unload the truck into their garage. The goal is to get the package to the destination the owner intended. We, like UPS, have temporary custody.

When my wife and I operated under the assumption that we could do whatever we pleased with "our" money without regard to God's desire, we were not good managers. We failed to ask the owner what his intentions were. We were operating under false assumptions. However, it doesn't matter whether we are ignorant of the principles when we break them. They exist without regard to our knowledge or our feelings about them. Like gravity, they are not negotiable. Flawed assumptions often result in unpleasant consequences.

In our culture, as your income increases, your lifestyle typically increases with it. We're told we deserve things. We buy newer, more excellent homes and newer, fancier cars and take frequent and more expensive vacations. Mostly financed with debt. In the Carolinas, where we live, an annual beach vacation is a necessity of life alongside food and water. One of the dangers of using debt to finance a better lifestyle is that it presumes that the future will be the same or better than the present. But the future is unknowable; in our case, we didn't expect problems with the home or the reversal in income. Who does? The Bible says, "The rich rule over the poor, and the borrower is slave to the lender" (Proverbs 22:7). That's exactly how we felt—slaves to the lender, in bondage to our home mortgage.

On January 25, 1998, during Super Bowl XXXII, we received and accepted an offer for our home. Finally! It was for $30,000 less than what we paid for it. The Denver Broncos defeated the Green Bay Packers that day. It seems odd to me when the results of the Super Bowl are reported in terms of one winner and one loser. Didn't both teams have to play a winning season and then become a league champion to play in the Super Bowl? In any case, we knew how the "losers" felt that day. Awful. The experience cost us a lot of stress, hardship, emotional pain, and tens of thousands of dollars. But we also had some sense of how the "winners" felt. We felt free. We felt lighter. Lighter but homeless!

We consider the financial cost of our experience as "tuition," an investment in our education. If we adapt our future behavior as a consequence, there is no need for self-flagellation, self-pity, or anger. The whole adventure was a powerful learning experience. Expensive tuition, to be sure, but also unforgettable and life-altering. The price of a master's degree from a heavenly university.

Hiking the entire Appalachian Trail is difficult, even if you can see where you are going. It is hard and, at times, brutal. Bill Irwin's trek on the trail often left him bruised and bloodied. He likely had no idea how his visit to our church and his story impacted us. He never knew us. Why would God ask a blind man to do something so ridiculous? I love Philip Yancey's definition of faith: believing in advance what only makes sense in reverse.[25] When God asked Bill and Orient to take that little walk, Bill never could have imagined how God would use it to influence others. Bill and Orient are no longer with us, but God still uses their story to reveal his ways and purposes. Our trials and tribulations while trying to sell this house were trivial compared to Bill's, but God was impressing us with the same principle:

We walk by faith, not by sight.

25 Philip Yancey, "The Long View," PhilipYancey.com, June 2023, https://philip yancey.com/the-long-view/

FINDING OUR PLACE
IN THE STORY

1. Nothing robs you of contentment like visiting model homes or watching home makeover television programs. True or false? How do you know?

2. Bill Irwin challenged everyone to consider whether we needed to lighten the load in our lives. What, if any, lifestyle changes could God be asking you to make?

3. The title of Bill Irwin's book is *Blind Courage*. We walk by faith and not by sight … it was more than just a Bible verse for Bill as he and Orient hiked the entire Appalachian Trail. How has this verse been true for you?

4. The scriptures reveal that God is the owner, controller, ruler, and distributor of everything in the heavens and the earth. Do you see yourself more like an owner or a manager? Give examples.

7

We Surrender

"If any man will come after me, let him deny himself,
and take up his cross daily, and follow me."

Luke 9:23 (KJV)

The cross of Christ didn't look like victory; surrender doesn't sound like freedom. Yet both of them are real for followers of Jesus. To surrender, capitulate, yield, or concede our will to God leads to freedom. It sounds counterintuitive because submitting to anything or anyone results in bondage. Jesus is the only exception. Every other person or idol will enslave us, but Jesus frees us. We learned this the "old-fashioned" way. The hard way.

After selling our nightmare home, we were given a little over two months to find a place to live. Resisting the cultural currents and leaning into biblical truth for direction, the next adventure was underway. On a recent Ken Boa podcast, he said, "The world will define you by default; the Word can only define you through discipline. Even a dead fish can float downstream."[26] His point is that if you're not biblically diligent and intentional, the culture will carry you to places you may not want to go. We resolved to walk by faith in this decision, wanting God's will ... no matter what!

---

26 Ken Boa, "Biblical Risk Taking: Leveraging the Temporal for Eternal Gain," 2019 Kingdom Advisors Conference breakout session, February 21, 2019, Orlando, FL.

The decision was a little more challenging because we invited my parents to share the next house with us part-time. Their primary home was in Florida, and the idea was for them to spend their summers with us in Charlotte. With this and other desires in mind, the perfect home should line up with six different "P's": payment, privacy, parking, produce, porch, and permission. We needed an affordable mortgage payment, reasonable privacy for both families, parking for four cars, space for a vegetable garden, a screened-in porch, and permission from the Lord to move ahead. Every potential option would be measured against these "s'P'ecifications."

The search began in earnest, and there wasn't much time. Before the internet, the only way to physically see inside a home was to tour it. We visited many houses, and it quickly became apparent that this would not be easy. "Easy-'P'easy" was not one of the "s'P'ecs." It was hard, tiring, and discouraging work. Thirty days before the April 15 closing was our self-imposed deadline, after which the plan was to move into a rental situation and continue searching. If God didn't move by that date, renting would be our answer.

Feeling discouraged as our deadline was almost upon us, we got down on our knees and prayed. Thanking God for his mercy and grace, we committed to renting for the time. We prayed that prayer that never fails: "Not my will but yours be done."[27] We would wait for him. We said our amens and got off our knees. The phone rang. Marlyn Jamison, our real estate agent, asked if we wanted to see one more house. It wasn't even on the market yet, but the sellers were open to letting us see it.

The house was a midcentury modern tri-level with ample parking, a garden, privacy, and a patio (almost a porch), and the price would support the level of payment we were comfortable with. It

---

27 Luke 22:42

seemed this was an answer to prayer in God's perfect timing. Sold! We've heard it said, "God is seldom early but never late." We're believers.

April 15, 1998, was the closing date on both homes. It took 1,437 days or three years, eleven months, and six days from our initial decision to sell the dream home until the day we moved into the perfect one. The Lord used this experience to do important transformation work in our hearts.

Perhaps one of this story's more surprising (to us) elements was our willingness to continue to wait on God. So often, our prayers feel like attempts to get God on our agenda, seeking his agreement with our will and timing instead of aligning our desires with his. This idea fits with what the Psalmist wrote, "Take delight in the Lord, and he will give you the desires of your heart" (Psalm 37:4). How else can you explain our 180-degree change of attitude? God was replacing old desires and agendas in our hearts with his desires and agenda. We were willing to wait longer to get his best for us. We trusted him and his timing more than our own. That was new. This was surrender. In the Kingdom of God, surrender is freedom. We felt free, and it was terrific.

We wanted the perfect home from his perspective. Two of the numbers in the Bible that relate to perfection are seven and twelve. For example, God's creation was complete on the seventh day. There are seven days in a week, seven Jewish holidays, and seven churches in the Book of Revelation. Jacob has twelve sons; they form the twelve tribes of Israel. Twelve minor prophets dot the text of the Old Testament. Jesus had twelve disciples, and there are twelve months in a year.

We believed we were living in the home he picked for us, and a few months after settling in our new home, God confirmed it. While driving to work, praying, and praising God, I meditated on the home's address, 712 Wingrave Drive. Read ... seven, twelve ... Win-over the grave ... of Jesus ... drive. No way! God cares about all aspects of our lives, even where we live. He answered our prayers and confirmed that this was the place he chose and prepared for us.

Surrendering fully to his will and plan was one of the best choices we've made. We were free from the bondage of our bad decisions, and we enjoyed a feeling of peace and freedom that can only come when we walk in obedience and submission. The house he chose for us, 712 Wingrave Drive ... was ideal regarding the payment, privacy, parking, produce, patio, and permission. Perfect.

FINDING OUR PLACE
IN THE STORY

1. Jesus challenges conventional wisdom. The cross of Christ doesn't look like victory, and surrender doesn't sound like freedom. How can this be true?

2. Every other person or idol will enslave us, but Jesus frees us. Can you think of examples for each of these?

3. "The world will define you by default; the Word can only define you through discipline. Even a dead fish can float downstream."[28] Can you identify the places the culture wants to carry you that you may not want to go or that aren't good for you?

4. Do your prayers feel like attempts to get God on your agenda? How can you seek alignment with his will and timing instead?

---

28 Ken Boa, "Biblical Risk Taking: Leveraging the Temporal for Eternal Gain," 2019 Kingdom Advisors Conference breakout session, February 21, 2019, Orlando, FL.

8

Getting Older Isn't for Sissies

"Honor your father and your mother, so that you may live
long in the land the LORD your God is giving you."

EXODUS 20:12

My mom was a complex person. She was the youngest child born to Croatian immigrants who came to the USA through Ellis Island at the turn of the twentieth century. She loved to read, was an incredible cook and baker, and had a playful sense of humor. Yet deep down in her wounded soul was a cauldron of contempt and anger that could erupt at any time.

Growing up, my brothers and I would warn each other when Mom was on the warpath. We learned to avoid her triggers. She said a lot of funny things that we still tell one another, like, "Getting older isn't for sissies." When we were being mischievous, she would say, "One day you are going to run after my coffin, and you know what, I'm not going to say a word." Or, "Your mother was a failure." On a bad day, her words could be quite destructive. One phrase she said to me with biting contempt many times when I was young was, "You make me sick." That still hurts.

My dad was on the other end of the complexity continuum.

He didn't read books but just looked at the pictures. He and his siblings grew up with a single mom after being abandoned by their father. He joined the Marines during WWII at the age of seventeen. He had a big servant's heart throughout his life. To make ends meet, he worked two jobs: a prison guard at the county penitentiary and a janitor in one of the local primary schools. He was fun to have around when he wasn't working and provided a good balance to Mom's outbursts. He loved games, especially cards, but you had to watch him closely because he enjoyed winning and wasn't afraid to cheat. He wasn't very good at charades or Trivial Pursuit, but his antics made the games unforgettable. He could be the life of the party or the equalizer. He was 50 percent Gramps and 50 percent Rambo … and 100 percent Grambo.

When we moved into 712 Wingrave Drive, the plan was for my parents, Carl and Tootie, to drive up from their Florida home and live with us during the summers. It was a chance for them to be closer to family, and it would benefit Kari. She had a great relationship with them. We were attempting a situation that would not be easy. I was especially concerned that it would be too hard for Sharon to have her in-laws under our roof for three or four months out of the year. Much prayer went into this, but God's grace gave us ten good summers together. Sharon was amazing, as always.

We have many fond memories from those summers together. We shared every evening meal, immediately followed by Pitch, our favorite card game. Our Pitch games were fast and loud. It was boys against girls, making Dad my partner, and I called him out for cheating at least once a day. No matter what we did, we spent a fair amount of time laughing.

My folks didn't sit around; they worked. I could hear my mom on the phone, telling my brothers that we had chained her to the stove, even though Sharon did as much cooking as she did. Dad loved to do projects inside and outside the house. There was not one room in our house that he hadn't helped make better. He was also a man with a mission outside, but the price for that help would include some collateral damage, as he was famous for breaking things. Carl and Tootie were good to us, and they were incredible grandparents. Kari flourished when they were around.

It's not easy to watch parents age, and leading up to what would have been our eleventh summer together, father time was rapidly closing in on them. We were about to have a front-row seat for what Mom meant when she said getting older wasn't for sissies. She had been in a lot of pain over the previous winter. We didn't know it, but her spine had compressed significantly, and she had lost four of five inches of height in a few short months. The doctor had her on some powerful painkillers. I didn't want Dad to make the drive that year and offered to fly down and drive with them, but he wouldn't let me.

On the day they were driving up, my phone rang. It was my mom calling from her cell. They had just been in an accident a few seconds before and were sitting in the car, waiting for the police. Dad had pulled out in front of a motorcycle, and the collision sent the rider crashing into their windshield and then over the other side. It was Dad's fault; they never saw him. A policeman at the scene got on the phone and told me he thought they were fine, but as a precaution, they were taking my parents to the hospital in Ocala, Florida. He said the car was undriveable. I got in my 2001 Toyota 4Runner and drove ten hours to get them.

Unfortunately, the man on the motorcycle was pronounced dead at the scene. We found out later that he was an off-duty deputy sheriff. Dad was cited for violation of the right of way. I had ten hours to process how this horrible event was going to change many lives. I couldn't begin to imagine the grief of the deputy's family. All we could do was pray for them and my parents. Ugh.

The next day, I found them at a local hotel, and I distinctly remember picking windshield glass from Mom's hair and shoes. We went to the place where they took the car to retrieve their clothes and other belongings. The car was a mangled mess, and the decimated Harley they had hit lay beside it. The drive back to Charlotte was intense, and Mom yelped in pain with every bump in the road. The 4Runner had good cargo space, but it wasn't the smoothest of rides. It was two of the worst days of our lives.

The next few weeks weren't much better. Dad was in denial, and Mom was in pain. Unable to do anything to please her, I was the target of a regular diet of criticism and condemnation. I know it was the pain and the medications, but she was unrelenting and uncooperative. It was pure hell. One day, she pushed me beyond my limit. It was around six in the morning; Sharon and I had just returned from walking the dog. As I walked by their bedroom, Mom asked to speak to me. I stood by her bed as she let me have it again. Before I knew what had happened, someone said to her with contemptuous venom, "You make me sick." That someone was me.

I was devastated and ashamed. I told Sharon what I had done and how awful I felt. It was like an out-of-body experience. But there it was, not only the very words she had spoken to me but also with all the anger and contempt I could muster. I have never said those words to anyone before or since. It was one of the worst moments of my life.

I was scheduled to go to Zambia on a three-week mission trip in a few weeks, but I knew I couldn't leave Sharon alone with the situation as it was. I called my brothers (Carl, Alan, and David), and they helped make arrangements to take over. By the time I returned from Africa, Mom and Dad had signed a lease for an apartment in Buffalo. They never returned to the Carolinas again and never returned to their home in Florida. That's not what we had in mind when we first moved into 712 Wingrave Drive. God had a different plan, and in a full-circle story, they ended their married life where it started … Buffalo, New York. My parents would never own another car, and Dad would never drive again.

It was a sad way to end an otherwise wonderful season. After that, we made many trips to visit them in Buffalo but never really spoke about what had happened. A few times, Mom volunteered that the painkillers had no adverse effects on her and that it was all my imagination. I chose not to engage in those discussions and just let it go. As I said, she was complex.

Their last years were spent in an over-fifty-five apartment complex that suited them well. Although it didn't offer many amenities, the people who lived there looked after one another, which was a beautiful example of what it looks like to love your neighbor. They were able to reconnect with old friends, neighbors, and relatives. My brother Dave and his family lived nearby and provided much support. Dad developed some dementia toward the end, but Mom stayed mentally sharp. We lost him on June 3, 2014, and Mom on June 9, 2018, almost exactly four years apart. Fittingly, their ashes are interred at St. Mary's in Swormville, where we grew up. Mom was right about one thing: getting older is not for sissies.

When I reflect on the good ten years in Charlotte and their final years in Buffalo, I realize we did live in the spirit of the commandment to honor your father and mother. And so did my brothers, each in our own way. My parents raised excellent men; we all married above our station. Sharon, Kari, and I are truly grateful for God's grace and many beautiful memories. It wasn't perfect, but it was good.

FINDING OUR PLACE
IN THE STORY

1. It's not easy to watch parents age, and getting older is not for sissies. What does/did honoring them look like in your context?

2. How would you like to be honored as a parent as you age? Does this story give you any ideas for making it easier for others to honor you?

3. What can you do now to be better prepared for getting older?

4. Family dynamics can be challenging. How have you seen God at work in those dynamics? Where have you experienced or relied on his grace during family gatherings?

9

"Heart Episode"

*"Carry each other's burdens, and in this way
you will fulfill the law of Christ."*

GALATIANS 6:2

"I'm in the emergency room," Sharon said over the telephone. "I know," I said, because I remembered she and others from our church had Stephen Ministries training scheduled at the hospital that evening. I had just gotten home from work, and Kari and I were on our own that night for dinner. "No," she said, "I am IN the emergency room. The doctor said I had an episode of the heart."

The call came on the evening of March 1, 2000. I was having a hard time processing what I was hearing. Sharon was in her forties and in excellent physical condition. We jogged together five times a week. She WAS NOT the poster child for heart trouble. A heart episode?

Kari and I have slightly different versions of that phone call. She was in nursing school at the time and howls with laughter when I say "heart episode" instead of heart attack. But that's how I remember it, and Sharon claims she doesn't know what she said. Sure. In any case, Kari and I gathered our wits and made our way to the hospital.

When we arrived, the doctors told us they were admitting Sharon for observation and more tests. Later that evening, the test results revealed elevated troponin and creatinine levels, confirming that Sharon did have an episode … I mean a heart attack.

Sharon IS the poster child for everything you should NOT do if you are a woman in her forties having chest pains. On the afternoon of March 1, the pressure began building in her arms and chest. She went for a walk with the dog, thinking that would help. It didn't. Then she tried to lie down, and even the dog was agitated and worried. When that didn't help, she decided to go ahead and drive herself to the hospital since she would have to be there later anyway. She parked the car as far away as possible, walked into the emergency room, and debated what to do next. (She told me she was "trying to walk it off." Walking is her cure for all maladies.) A nurse asked her if she needed help. Sharon told her she was thinking about it and she was having chest pains. The nurse signed her in and told her to go sit down. They left her there, having chest pains, for the next two hours. You can't make this stuff up.

When our pastor, Steve Cathcart, saw Sharon missing from the Stephen Ministries meeting, he searched and found her in the emergency room's waiting area, still in pain. He sprung into action and finally got her help, but the symptoms were subsiding by now. Steve went back to check on the Stephen Ministers in training. Soon, the word spread throughout our church fellowship that Sharon was in the hospital because of a heart episode. (Sorry, Kari.)

This was the first time we had been on the receiving end of the remarkable ability of the body of Christ to bear one another's burdens and fulfill the law of Christ. The love, concern, and support from our church family astounded us. We felt like a "love cocoon" had been wrapped around our little family. I've heard people say they "felt" prayers, and now we know what they meant.

When you hear "hospital" and "heart attack," most minds gravitate toward the worst-case scenarios. This, thankfully, was not one of those. Sharon had a mild heart attack and minimal damage. Her episode was the result of losing the heart DNA lottery with a family history of heart disease. Sharon's father and older sister both had heart trouble.

Many from our church began coming to the hospital to check on us. As each one walked gingerly into the room, expecting the worst, you could see the shock on their faces when confronted with the patient sitting up in bed, talking, laughing, and looking … great. At times, it got very crowded and quite loud in that small room. The nurses came in and told us to keep it down because the noise made it hard for them to do their jobs.

Sharon was released from her detention after completing a heart catheterization. Her instructions were to back off the jogging for a while. We discovered the joy of walking and decided to make that our new cardio exercise, which we continue to this day.

We were truly grateful for how our church family rallied around us during this scare. Our birth families are hundreds of miles away with lives of their own, but as followers of Jesus, we have brothers and sisters everywhere we go. And because of them and the Holy Spirit, we are never alone or without help. It gives us a sense of peace, and our hearts overflow with gratitude.

There were many lessons learned through this scare. The most important one is that if you see my beautiful bride out walking alone … feel free to call 911. She's probably trying to "walk off" the next heart episode.

FINDING OUR PLACE
IN THE STORY

1. It is not unusual for women's heart issues to be discounted. Can you think of one or two takeaways from this story for application in a health crisis?

2. Do you live near relatives or far away from them? Have you ever been in a position to be blessed by a family of faith in a difficult time? What happened? How did it make you feel?

3. Could God be asking you to serve as the "family" to someone who lives far away from relatives? Make a prospective list and pray through it.

4. When we long to belong to a loving community, sometimes the best way to find one is to create one. Can you think of anyone who would join you in such an endeavor?

10

Trust Matters

*"Trust in the LORD with all your heart and lean not on
your own understanding; in all your ways submit to
him, and he will make your paths straight."*

PROVERBS 3:5–6

F ollowers of Jesus believe that a heavenly future awaits us when
we die. Beyond that, there is a future with him in a new heaven
and earth.[29] We take it on faith, which means trusting that he can
and will do what he has promised. We all must ask and answer the
question: Is what or who I'm putting my faith in trustworthy? It
occurred to me that perhaps the best way to answer the question
would be to try to live by faith. I didn't want to wait until I died and
be surprised. While I was still breathing, I wanted to get to know
him and see if he could be trusted. Raising the dead seems like it
would be hard to do. I wanted to know if I could trust him to do
it. Don't you?

Someone told me faith is spelled R I S K. I promise you, whoever did undoubtedly knew something about F E A R. I've lived
with fear as a constant companion all my life. I bet you have, too.
Taking risks was something I had to learn to do even before I
became a follower of Jesus.

---

29 Revelation 21:1

I wasn't born with the "risk gene." My parents were card-carrying members of the "greatest generation." The Great Depression and WWII shaped their lives and their thinking. By the time they had their four boys, safety and security were at the top of their minds and hearts. I mentioned that our dad worked two jobs during a significant swath of our growing-up years, and his primary job was as a prison guard. He was a civil servant, which we learned meant you had health insurance and a pension plan and didn't go on strike. It's how they spelled S A F E T Y.

My brothers and I are products of the post-WWII baby boom. If you didn't grow up in the '50s and '60s, a good depiction of what life was like back then is the TV series "The Wonder Years." We played outdoors without parental supervision, drank well water out of a dirty hose, and made up our fun. When we fought with each other or the neighbors, we settled things on our own. A baseball bat doubled as a bazooka, and corn cobs were grenades. We lived through the Martin Luther King Jr. and both Kennedy assassinations, the Vietnam War, and Watergate. We were taught to fear a good many things, like nuclear war with Russia, and worse things, like Republicans (according to my parents' political view at the time). Money, or its scarcity, always worried Mom. During the Depression, Mom's family lost their home, which profoundly impacted her, and through her anxiety, we were influenced.

I said I wasn't born with the "risk gene," but it may have laid dormant. Our maternal grandparents were big-time risk-takers, emigrating from Croatia at the turn of the twentieth century. They came through Ellis Island with nothing. No English, job, health insurance, pension ... nothing. Nothing but a dream and hope for a better life. I wish I had asked them how their faith had influenced their decision. They were devout Catholics.

At some point early on, we all wrestle with questions about what we will do with the rest of our lives. I had no clue what I was made for. However, one overriding belief that drove me forward was that if I continued to live at home, my life would be awful. Everything looked better than terrible. At nineteen, I left the only home I had ever known for the wilderness of Wisconsin and the hope of finding a new life. I went to Milwaukee, which isn't the wilderness, but most think Wisconsin is in the hinterlands. I blame the cheeseheads.

It was not quite the leap of faith my maternal grandparents took, but it was my first considerable life risk. At least I had health insurance, could speak "Wisconsinese," and liked cheese … so I had those going for me. My worldly possessions fit into my yellow 1971 AMC Hornet, and I drove the 680 miles to and through Chicago, ending up in Milwaukee. Driving that distance alone was a big hurdle, but negotiating the traffic through the Windy City felt monumental. It was terrifying. This was just the beginning of a pattern of risk-taking that would define my young life. There were some reasonable risks and some not-so-reasonable, but all the risks challenged and frightened me.

When the pain of your current reality is greater than the pain (fear) of some other uncertain future reality, the answer equals: it's time to make a change. It feels like a math problem. As I've grown older, the answers to life's many challenges and choices have morphed into the math equations I hated as a student. When in doubt, do the math. Then, rinse and repeat. But what do you do when your options and reality create paralyzing fear? It happened to the Israelites several times in their history, most notably when the Lord told Moses to send out spies from each tribe to explore Canaan. This was the Promised Land, a land reported to be flowing with milk and honey. Upon their return, ten of those spies were overcome by fear. "We can't attack those people! They're too strong for us! The land we explored is one that devours those who live there. All the people we saw there are very tall. We felt as small as grasshoppers, and that is how we must have looked to them."[30]

Only two spies, Joshua and Caleb, disagreed with the others. They didn't say their reports were inaccurate, but their faith and trust in God gave them confidence and courage. But fear won the day, and the Israelites refused to go. Their fear was so pronounced that the thought of going back to slavery in Egypt looked good to them. The Israelites would continue to wander in the desert for their lack of faith. Only Joshua and Caleb, from that generation, were allowed to enter Canaan forty years later.[31]

It's tempting to be critical and judgmental of the faith failures of others, especially the characters we learn about in the scriptures. Perhaps that's a symptom of pride. There is nothing quite like a personal episode of paralyzing fear to inject a dose of humility into one's life. In the fall of 2000, God would bring me to my Canaan experience.

At this point, I was forty-five years old and had been following Jesus earnestly for seven years. Sharon and I had been married for almost seventeen years, and during that time, there were many career moves and location changes. The financial services world vastly differed from when I had entered it twenty years before. In 1980, there were no PCs or the internet. The world was evolving at a faster and faster pace. The rules of commerce and careers were changing with it. I had imagined a career in support roles for those in the retail side of financial services. The one thing I knew I could never do was become a financial advisor. This was unobtainable

30 Numbers 13:31–33
31 Numbers 14:6–24

and unreachable because I couldn't prospect and sell. But God, evidently, was leading me along a different path. A path with giants so big I felt like a grasshopper in comparison.

Have you ever been so afraid to attempt an activity that you would rather die than face that fear? I did, and it's unpleasant, debilitating, and humiliating. It was more than just being afraid to fail, although it was certainly that. No, my fear was rational because I knew I couldn't do it. And I was right.

Sharon and I were at an unpleasant crossroads as a family, and I needed a job. The only opportunity at the time was working at Carroll Financial, in my opinion, one of the best financial planning firms in the country. It is humiliating when you know you don't belong, don't fit, and aren't ready. All those things were true.

Larry Carroll, the managing partner, offered me an opportunity. For the next twelve months, I would work for him for a part-time salary and work for myself part-time. If you put the two together, you have a full-time job. When I wasn't helping Larry, I was free to see if I could succeed at prospecting and building a client base—no promises beyond the next twelve months.

At forty-five, I was starting over and creating a career from scratch. In the days leading up to working there and for some time after, fear and I were constant companions. The mental anguish was excruciating. One night, when I couldn't sleep, with tears streaming down my face, I prayed for death to come so I wouldn't have to face another day. A request that I am grateful God didn't agree to.

Like the Israelites, my problem wasn't in assessing the risk. We were both spot-on in all of it. Our fears grew out of a lack of faith and trust. Unlike the Israelites, however, I did move forward. It was really, really hard, but his grace was sufficient for me. Each day, I showed up and did what I knew to do, and God's grace was manna to me ... enough for one day at a time. Days turned into weeks and weeks into months. At the end of one year, I went into Larry's office to see where I stood. By the look on his face, I could tell he didn't remember his twelve-month condition. He told me, "You're good for another thirty days." And that's the way it's been for the last twenty-three years (276 months and counting).

As time passed, the Lord and I developed an extraordinary partnership. It took me a few years to figure it out, but he didn't call me to the financial planning business to prospect. God had something much better in mind. In our partnership, he brought in the prospects, and my job was to help each one with their financial needs and love them well. I know now that this experience was not about building a business. The business was a means to an end, perhaps several of them. Twenty-three years later, I see he was increasing my faith and strengthening our relationship. And a lot of people got helped and loved in the process. He was teaching me that I could trust him. Trust Matters.®

Follow the Thread

George MacDonald's children's book *The Princess and the Goblin* helped me better understand the challenge of following Jesus into fearful places.[32]

Irene, the protagonist in the story, is eight years old. She found an attic room in her house, and every so often, her fairy grandmother appears there. When Irene goes to look for her, she's usually not there, so one day, her fairy grandmother gives her a ring with a thread tied to it, leading to a little ball of thread. She explains that she'll keep the ball. "But I can't see it," says Irene. "No. The

---

32 "George MacDonald's children's book The Princes and the Goblin" : George MacDonald, *The Princess and the Goblin* (Chicago, IL: Cannonball Books, 2020).

thread is too fine for you to see it. You can only feel it." With this reassurance, Irene tests the thread.

"Now listen," says the fairy grandmother, "if you ever find yourself in danger … you must take off your ring and put it under the pillow of your bed. Then you must lay your forefinger … upon the thread, and follow the thread wherever it leads you."

"Oh, how delightful! It will lead me to you, Grandmother, I know!"

"Yes," said the grandmother, "but remember, it may seem to you a very roundabout way indeed, and you must not doubt the thread. Of one thing you may be sure, that while you hold it, I hold it too."

In MacDonald's telling, the goblins get into Irene's house, and she takes off her ring and puts it under the pillow. She begins to feel the thread, but to her dismay, it takes her right toward the goblins' cave. She tries to follow the thread backward but discovers the thread only works forward, and forward now leads to a wall of stones. She begins tearing it down stone by stone and suddenly hears the voice of her friend Curdie, who has been trapped in the goblin's cave. Irene's grandmother led her there so she could rescue Curdie, and after some convincing, Curdie and Irene followed the thread to safety together. The thread proves reliable because her grandmother is trustworthy.

The thread story captured the essence of what I experienced as I was compelled to move forward in a way that I didn't want to go in my career. It's hard to follow someone or something that you can't see. Carroll Financial seemed a roundabout way to me then, just like Irene's path. I couldn't see how anything good was going to happen. It was all so dark. But God is more powerful than our giants, and he is good. He is worthy of our trust.

"Following the thread" can take you to hard places. Every hard place has a purpose and is used by God in ways we've never dreamed about. We have no idea how our lives affect the lives of others, but we will have all of eternity to hear the stories. That's going to be a blast.

The thread in MacDonald's story only worked forward, and because the world turns on its axis, the shortest and quickest way to the dawn is toward the darkness, not away from it. This is also true of fear. The shortest and best way to triumph over any fear is to turn toward it and enter into it. Jesus looked at his cross in the same way, and he is asking us to follow him despite our fears. A lifetime of following the invisible Jesus will give us the confidence that he has the will and the power to raise our bodies from the dead. He is trustworthy, and he is faithful. Trust Matters®.

FINDING OUR PLACE
IN THE STORY

1. "Someone told me faith is spelled R I S K. I promise you, whoever did undoubtedly knew something about F E A R." What does that mean to you?

2. Have you had a Canaan or wilderness experience? What was it like? What did you learn?

3. Have you ever been so afraid to attempt an activity that you would rather die than face that fear? How do you overcome fear?

4. "As time passed, the Lord and I developed an extraordinary partnership." How do you see yourself partnering with God in your daily life?

5. "You must not doubt the thread. Of one thing you may be sure, that while you hold it, I hold it too."[33] How do you see yourself in the story of *The Princess and the Goblin*?

---

33 George MacDonald, *The Princess and the Goblin* (Chicago, IL: Cannonball Books, 2020).

11

Adoption

*"The Spirit you received does not make you slaves, so that you
live in fear again; rather, the Spirit you received brought about
your adoption to sonship. And by him we cry, 'Abba, Father.'"*

ROMANS 8:15

After Sharon, Kari, and I became a family, we considered adding
to our number. I loved being a dad to Kari, and we wanted her
to grow up with siblings like we did. Unfortunately, we were not
able to have more biological children, which bothered me for a
long time and saddened me. There would never be a Mike Jr. or a
Betty Jette to join our clan. (It was rumored my dad always wanted
a Betty Jette.) We discussed the idea of adoption and were open to
it. My brother Alan and his wife, the "other and first Sharon Jette,"
adopted twice. We knew we could go to them for help and advice.

We committed the adoption idea to prayer. One of the life
lessons we learned from past mistakes was to be careful when
making big decisions and to examine our motives. It is easy to
deceive yourself, and bad decisions lead to consequences that
are always unpleasant. We wanted God's will for us. "There are
millions of unwanted children all over the world; help as many as
you want," said a voice inside me. This truth was foundational to

our exploration of helping orphans in developing nations, and it initiated fresh thinking about our legacy and what it meant to be a family.

Sometimes, people said hurtful things to me about our family. They made it a point to refer to Kari as "Sharon's daughter," emphasizing that, in their eyes, I was not her "real dad," and we were not a real family. It was the same when our grandson, Chase, was born. He was Sharon's grandson, not ours. The words came with a false smile and sometimes concluded with, "Bless your heart." Could it be that there is more to being a family than biology? Is there more to a legacy than your place on the family tree? Jesus asked, "Who is my mother, and who are my brothers?" Then he looked at those seated in a circle around him and said, "Here are my mother and my brothers. For whoever does the will of my Father in heaven is my brother and sister and mother."[34] Jesus thought there was more to being a family than our biological DNA.

Jesus had a more expansive and inclusive definition of family. He chose to spend three years of his short life pouring into twelve people he selected. And of those, he picked three to be in his inner circle: Peter, James, and John. The book of Hebrews, chapter 10, verse 19, says we are brothers and sisters in God's family because of the blood of Jesus. Followers of Jesus are brothers and sisters. That is one big family! Pastor Chuck Swindoll taught, "There are only two eternal things on earth today. Only two: people and God's Word."[35] These truths have profound implications for us and exciting opportunities. It's clear from the Romans 8:15 passage that

34 Matthew 12:46–50
35 Pastor Chuck Swindoll, "What Lasts Forever? Only Two Things," The Bible-Teaching Ministry of Paster Chuck Swindoll, Article Library, insight.org, July 8, 2015, https://insight.org/resources/article-library/individual/what-lasts-forever-only-two-things.

God sees us as his adopted children, part of his forever family. Our Abba!

There is more than one way to be a family. Looking through the lens of eternity, I began to see family everywhere. There are birth, work, and spiritual families, and God has given me a unique extended family. These relationships are gifts from God and precious to him and to me, pregnant with eternal possibilities. Bob Goff spoke at a conference I attended and said, "Around your deathbed, you have room for eight people … nine if they're skinny."[36] Then he went on to ask, "Who are your nine? Do they know it?" It's a powerful image, and it had an immediate impact on me. Bob illustrated what Jesus had done in asking the twelve to follow him.

My extended family are those I envision around my deathbed, and they have a special place in my life for many reasons. I found it helpful to think of them this way because I can intentionally invest more time and energy into these relationships. Your extended family comprises the people you want to impact the most for eternity. It includes birth and biological relatives but is intended to be much more expansive.

One of the people in that inner circle is Eric deNeve. Eric no longer walks among us but waits for me on the other side. Before he died, he promised he would be there to greet me upon my arrival. Eric will be unseen around my deathbed but present. Another of the nine is Ben Ganson. God used Eric to connect Ben and me. The deNeve, Ganson, and Jette families have experienced unique and unexpected God adventures together.

---

36 Bob Goff, "Love Does," Kingdom Advisors Conference, February 2015, Orlando, Florida, https://sunset.kingdomadvisors.com/resources/love-does.

Ganson Family

In 2013, the Gansons and four other families moved from Ohio to Rock Hill, South Carolina, to plant a Vineyard Church. Sharon and I moved to Rock Hill from Charlotte in 2014, and we were looking for a new church home. Eric met Rachel, a young woman working at his favorite Panera Bread restaurant, and she was part of the Rock Hill Vineyard church planting team. Their conversation prompted him to email me about a new church in our area. He wrote, "It sounds like the church we've always wanted to belong to." I deleted the email and forgot about it.

After a few days, something stirred inside me, and I began to feel bad about deleting Eric's email. I rescued it from the deleted bin and reread it. Not every email deserves to be saved, but this one did. It seems God can speak to us through other people and even email. I looked at the church website and sent a message to the lead staff member, Ben Ganson. After trading emails, we decided to meet for lunch.

Ben and I had an instant rapport, even though I was old enough to be his father. Finding a new church home wasn't something Sharon and I had done in twenty-five years, and we didn't know anything about the Vineyard movement. I had been a leader in the Presbyterian church we attended for most of those years. My only other church experience was the Roman Catholic tradition of my youth. Vineyard was not like either of those, and I suppose that's what prompted Eric's email and piqued my curiosity.

We live in a hyper-consumer-oriented culture; unfortunately, this paradigm has infiltrated the church. People tend to "shop" for churches as they shop for cars. They come with a list of requirements, like a specific type of worship music, children and youth programs, charismatic leaders, and entertaining sermons. And when the church falls out of fashion, the search begins for another. At the bottom of the list, but mostly missing, is the consideration of where God is leading them. We resisted that approach and asked God, "Where do you want us in this next season of life?"

We did our due diligence. We prayed, read, and researched, and I regularly met with Ben. I learned why Eric thought Rock Hill Vineyard was for us in those conversations. It would not be focused on concepts I learned to despise ... the ABCs of "Churchianity": attendance, buildings, and cash. As lead pastor, Ben would be a "tent-maker." The name comes from the Apostle Paul, who earned an income from his tent-making work to finance the preaching of the gospel. Pastor and church staff salaries, building construction, and maintenance typically consume most of a church's budget. In my experience, they dominate much of the leadership's time and energy. Rock Hill Vineyard, at conception, would be free from the shackles and distractions of the ABCs.

The church was so new that it hadn't even begun meeting yet, but we were there when the doors opened in October 2014 at the local YMCA. Ten years later, we are still there. We don't meet at the Y now but at each other's homes.

In early 2015, I invited Ben to have lunch. At the time, he was working part-time at a local sign shop. I told him, "I have an idea, but I don't know if it's good. Would you consider quitting your job at the sign shop to come and work with me in my practice?" I thought his talents might be better used in the financial planning world. He had a college degree in business, and I could see he was good at planning from how he started and managed our church. I needed good part-time help, and after several failed attempts at hiring someone like-minded, hiring Ben seemed like a good idea. I thought it could be a win-win.

Sharon and I took Ben and his wife, Janelle, to dinner to discuss it. We wanted to give them answers to all their questions and concerns. After dinner, it still "seemed" like a good idea. But to allow God to bless or kill it, I wanted Ben to interview with higher-ups in our firm. If they told me, "Don't do it," I would let the idea drop. He interviewed with them, and they said, "Go." We did … and we are still going. Ben is a full-time Certified Financial Planner and has become the lead advisor on our team. He is still tent-making.

I love how God connects people to accomplish his purposes. A woman named Rachel joins a group leaving Ohio to plant a church in South Carolina. She tells a Panera customer named Eric about the new church. Eric sends his friend Mike an email, and Mike emails pastor Ben. And the adventure begins!

Haiti

One of our first endeavors as a church was to partner with The Outreach Foundation (TOF), a mission organization where I was a trustee. TOF was sending a group on a four-day vision trip to Cite Soleil, Haiti. Our group included Tom Widmer and Rick Wesley representing TOF, my friend Lans Slack, and four church members: Janelle Ganson, Lindsey Bucher, Sharon Jette, and me. Our purpose in going was to see if God was leading us to partner with Haiti Outreach Ministries (HOM).

HOM Founding Director Leon Dorleans began preaching in Cite Soleil, one of the poorest slums in Port-au-Prince, in 1989. Pastor Leon's vision was to address the spiritual, educational, and healthcare needs of the residents of Cite Soleil.

In our time with Pastor Leon in Haiti, he shared the challenges and struggles of living and working there. We witnessed the extremes of unspeakable poverty and unbridled worship and love for God. It was both heartbreaking and inspiring. One of the most distressing scenes was of the young mothers baking mud cookies in the outdoor sun to feed their children. Cookies made of clay, butter, and salt are a traditional remedy for hunger and are even considered to have health benefits—the clay contains minerals such as calcium. But they can also contain germs and toxins, and depending on these dirt cookies for sustenance can lead to malnutrition. It made a lasting impression.

During our stay in Haiti, Janelle felt a strong tug on her heart that the Lord wanted her and Ben to adjust their adoption plans. She thought he was saying to forgo their plan for domestic adoption and switch their focus to international. Specifically, he wanted them to consider adopting two children from Haiti. I wish I could have been a fly on the wall for that conversation when Janelle got home. "Hey honey, we had a great trip to Haiti, and oh, by the way, we are going to adopt two Haitian kids."

The Gansons need to tell their adoption story, and I could not do it justice. From what I witnessed, it should be a book to capture all the obstacles and subsequent miracles. International adoption is hard. Transnational adoption from Haiti is almost impossible. The time from our vision trip to the consummation of the adoption would be seven long years. During that time, Haiti would experience an earthquake, hurricane, presidential assassination, and gang takeover of the country.

One of the biggest challenges for followers of Jesus is to trust his timing. Ask Abraham and Sarah (Genesis 15–21). Why would God wait seven years to fulfill Ben and Janelle's desire to rescue two children from a life with little hope and opportunity? Someone said, "Faith is believing in advance what only makes sense in reverse." I like that definition. I hope Ben and Janelle publish their story. On

October 11, 2022, three-and-a-half-year-old twins Marvens and Marvel Ganson joined their forever family.

Ben, Janelle, Micah, Caleb, Abby, Marvens, and Marvel are now too many to fit around my deathbed. They fill up seven of the nine slots just by themselves. I will have to get a much bigger bed. They are family. We've "adopted" them and others. Bob Goff said, "I used to think following God required a lot of navigation, but now I know all I need is a line and a circle. Grace draws a circle around everyone and says they're in."[37] Works for me.

God is always showing up for us in the small things. We don't always hear his voice, and it is easy to miss much of what he is up to around us. Sometimes, he talks to us through deleted emails, but our failures won't prevent him from accomplishing his will. He adopts us and connects us in communities he calls family. Grace draws a circle around everyone and says they're in. May the size of all our families' circles continue to increase.

---

37 Bob Goff, *Love Does: Discover a Secretly Incredible Life in an Ordinary World* (Nashville, TN: Thomas Nelson, 2012).

FINDING OUR PLACE
IN THE STORY

1. "Be careful when making big decisions and examine your motives. It is easy to deceive yourself, and bad decisions lead to unpleasant consequences." What do you think about committing decisions to prayer before moving forward?

2. "Jesus thought there was more to being a family than our biological DNA." How can this apply to your life?

3. "God sees us as his adopted children, part of his forever family. Our Abba!" How are we adopted into God's family? Do you know him as "Abba"?

4. "Around your deathbed, you have room for eight people … nine if they're skinny."[38] Who are your nine? Do they know it?

5. "We live in a hyper-consumer-oriented culture; unfortunately, this paradigm has infiltrated the church. People tend to 'shop' for churches as they shop for cars." How should we find our church family?

6. "Grace draws a circle around everyone and says they're in."[39] Identify all the families you are a part of and make a list.

38 Bob Goff, "Love Does," Kingdom Advisors Conference, February 2015, Orlando, Florida, https://sunset.kingdomadvisors.com/resources/love-does.

39 Bob Goff (@bobgoff), "Grace draws a circle around all of us and says we're in," X.com, January 26, 2018, 9:18 AM, https://x.com/bobgoff/status/95692422 3687081984.

12

Ministry of Presence

"But Moses said, 'Pardon your servant,
Lord. Please send someone else.'"

Exodus 4:13

In the Exodus story, God speaks to Moses through a burning bush. That would get my attention. Still, Moses is reluctant to take on what is being asked of him. Over the years, I would be asked to go places I didn't want to—some near and some far. I learned many insights from these experiences, but two lessons are the most valuable. First, over time, without exception, when I obeyed God and went where he asked me to go, I never regretted it. I always received a measure of joy and satisfaction. I could feel God's pleasure. If that weren't enough, God would reveal truths about himself to me, and our relationship would grow stronger. Whenever I said, "No, please send someone else," I always regretted it. There wasn't condemnation, only grace, but no joy, either. Second, showing up for others in difficult places is a profound blessing and mystery. People have expressed profound gratitude to God for our showing up wherever we've gone. Don't miss that nuance; they always thanked God first. They felt loved and seen by him. It's the ministry of presence, simple but powerful, and it would take me to places across town, the country, and the ocean. One of God's most challenging "asks" was the invitation to follow him to Africa.

Travel is romanticized in our culture. Travel companies spend billions annually on digital, print, and television advertising. They have to because we all know traveling can be horrible. I wouldn't say I like it. For me, it ranks up there with a root canal. I relate international travel to having a colonoscopy. The thought of either one gives me ... well, you get the picture. They didn't call me "the anchor" of this relationship for nothing. The chances of my choosing to go to Africa were akin to a snowball's chance in Hades.

I don't have a bucket list, and Africa would not have been on it if I did. If you ever wondered if God has a sense of humor, consider as evidence that I would travel back and forth to southern Africa enough times that I lost count. I suspect the final number was around fifteen. As time went on, Africa and I developed a love-hate relationship. I hated the travel, homesickness, anxiety, and constant feeling of not being enough. There was not a time when I didn't feel in over my head, and there was one time I got so sick I thought I would die. Seriously! My body wasn't equipped for African viruses. I loved the people, the wisdom I was learning, and how I grew. I loved going on safaris. Safaris are the one thing I would put on a bucket list. You should, too. Please do it now; I'll wait.

Why Africa?

As our twenty-fifth wedding anniversary approached, Sharon and I tried to decide how to celebrate. Because we were cultivating a biblical worldview, we considered ideas that would last beyond the temporal. How could we celebrate in a way that expressed our gratitude to God for twenty-five years of married life and blessed someone else simultaneously? (BOGO, see chapter 26, "The Lost Gospel of Jettekiah.") Curious things began to happen to us.

At a Christian conference in Atlanta, we were introduced to and entertained by a choir of orphans from Africa. It was both worshipful and heartbreaking. These kids made an impression. After we returned home, Africa or orphan needs were brought to our attention everywhere we turned. Random letters and brochures came in the mail, or that's how it seemed. Was God trying to tell us something? We began praying earnestly for guidance and direction. We also told other friends about this burden and asked them to pray. Was this an invitation from him to join in some Kingdom work?

While praying and waiting for his answer, we decided to take a small step and sponsor an orphan from the organization that brought the choir to Atlanta. We looked through their materials and picked a child whose name was Caleb. We were drawn to his name because Caleb, an Old Testament hero, was one of the two spies who trusted God and believed he would deliver Canaan into Israel's hands. This Caleb was from a country called Zambia. I'd never heard of it, but it sounded African, and he was our guy.

Do You Want to Go to Zambia?

On April 2, 2008, while attending a Wednesday evening church supper, Doug Vinez, the guest speaker, was dining across the table from us. (Who knew church suppers were so dangerous?) Doug and his wife, Abby, had attended our church years ago, and we spent most of the dinner getting reacquainted. He asked, "What is the church doing in international missions?"

"Nothing."

"Too bad, so do you want to go to Zambia?"

"Yes!"

That's just how it happened. There was no hesitation on my part because there was no doubt in my mind that God was opening the door. Also, Sharon put her fingers in her ears to block out the conversation, so that was another clue.

Doug and Abby were returning to Zambia on a short-term mission trip with a small group from a few churches north of Charlotte. Two people had just dropped out. I would take one of the spots, and my good friend Eric deNeve would take the other. Eric and his wife, Jan, were the friends who had committed to praying with us about Africa, and they witnessed the conversation with Doug at that supper. (I later shared this story at Eric's memorial service.)

I had never dreamed of going to Africa until that night. Not once. Our thoughts for helping were about writing checks. That night, I looked at a map of Africa to see where Zambia was. Zambia was out of this hemisphere and out of my comfort zone. There was much to do and much to learn in a short amount of time. The team was leaving on July 1.

Up to that point, I had participated in a few short-term mission trips with our church. Only one had been out of the country, and it was to Jamaica, which wasn't far, and English was the primary language. Going to Zambia required vaccinations, malaria medications, and multiple travel days with long flights and challenging layovers. The entire trip would be nineteen days, and I had never been away from home for that long in our twenty-five years as a couple.

Toto, I've a Feeling We Aren't in Kansas Anymore

Our final destination was Mwandi, Zambia, a small village bordering the Zambezi River in the Western Province, about seventy-five miles west of Livingstone and Victoria Falls. At times, as many as eight thousand people call Mwandi home.[40] The people are mainly

---

40 "Welcome to the Mwandi OVC Project!" Mwandi OVC Project (homepage), accessed July 25, 2024, https://mwandiovcproject.com/.

of the Lozi tribe, semi-nomadic cattle herders and fishermen. They live in mud huts, their infrastructure is poor, and electricity and clean water are not readily available, though recent development efforts have begun to change that. Most families live on less than $3 daily.

For the group, this was a short-term mission trip, but for me, this was an answer to prayer and more of a vision trip. I hoped to see if there was something in that area for the Jettes to do as an anniversary blessing, but I couldn't imagine what that could be. We know that following Jesus requires a lot of walking by faith, and we've learned to lean into it instead of away from it. We were headed to Africa. This felt more like running by faith.

Eric and I were latecomers to the team, but it didn't take long for us to find our place among the fifteen others. After two long days of travel, Zambia was within sight. As our plane approached the Livingstone airport, Eric took a great picture of Victoria Falls below us. We looked down on one of the world's seven wonders and would stand next to it in a few days. This was just the first of many new realities to bombard our senses. For me, landing in Zambia was similar to landing on the moon. It felt like we were in a different world. Things looked different, smelled different, sounded different, felt different, and tasted different. I'm sure it's how Dorothy felt when she landed in Oz.

Rury and Fiona Waddell

Rury and Fiona were full-time missionaries living in Mwandi. Before they were married, Fiona started the Orphan and Vulnerable Children Project (OVC). When their children Lucy and Cora were born, we became their Uncle Mike and Auntie Sharon—proudly worn titles. I have made room for the Waddells around my deathbed. I call Rury my younger-older brother. I learned much from Rury; he showed me how to live and thrive in Mwandi. I always felt safer when he was around. He is Scottish and studied and trained to be an attorney, but his passion has always been fishing, animal husbandry, and agriculture.

There were no "typical" days while on a mission in Africa. Each day was unique, presenting us with various challenges and opportunities. On one memorable day, Rury asked some team members to join him in an agricultural service project for Skuzu, a nearby village.

The service project was deworming cattle. Keeping the animals healthy is essential work. Toby, one of the team members, was a veterinarian, so he was very popular, and they kept him very busy. But what does a Certified Financial Planner have to offer a crew of cattle-rustling Zambians? Not much … but as a regulatory precaution, when I was invited to join the deworming party, I ensured I had a prospectus and all the proper disclosure documents. You just had to know how much the team was looking forward to my helping them on this day.

Skuzu is a neighboring village about four miles east of Mwandi, accessible only by foot or four-wheel drive vehicle through the bush. The population of Skuzu is unknown but is thought to be about two hundred to three hundred. Their children go to school in Mwandi, walking the four miles each way through the bush. Can you imagine sending your first grader off to school each day in that scenario?

Rury drove us in a Land Rover loaded with our veterinarian supplies. Our mission was to examine three hundred bulls and cows. The cattle are the village's primary revenue source, and we treated them that day for several diseases, the most common of which is worms. These cattle are to the people what our paychecks and investment portfolios are to us. To some extent, the cattle are their status, wealth, and power. (Compliance restrictions do not allow me to develop this metaphor further, but hopefully, you get the idea.)

As we climbed into the vehicle and began our trek, Doug Vinez's daughter Emily offered to sit between Toby and me. *How sweet*, I thought, until I realized that the Rover's window was broken and locked in the down position. There is no road to Skuzu, only sand, potholes, and brush, and most of that seemed to swipe against our vehicle and then slap me in the face with fantastic accuracy as we drove through it. How sweet and thoughtful was our Emily?

Arriving in Skuzu, we visited the first of four kraals (enclosures) and one cattle crush. That's when the real fun began. The cattle owners and their sons started a "dance" that we could not have imagined before, but we would see it repeated 121 times before the day was over. To treat the animal, they had to wrestle it to the ground. This dance took an average of three men for these large cows and bulls ... one trying to put a rope on the head, one attempting to rope the back feet, and one pulling the animal down to the ground by its tail. All in the context of a tiny space, with many horns and hoofs extremely agitated and constantly moving. The phrase "Look out behind you, Toby" was often heard.

In case you were wondering what my job was, as luck would have it, no one thought to hire a photographer. As much as I was looking forward to putting my hand in a bull's nose like Toby seemed to enjoy doing ... well, darn it ... I got stuck taking pictures and filling syringes with deworming medicine. A job I became quite accomplished at, by the way, around the 120th cow.

When we finished our work, we returned to the mission house where we stayed. That night, we shared a couple of Mosi beers and a few good laughs. As a financial planner, the best news of the day was the realization that we had seen hundreds of bulls and not one bear!

Someone once said, "God isn't interested in your abilities but your availability." That's the definition of the ministry of presence ... being available. We followed Jesus to Africa, believing he would give us a vision of what he wanted us to do. We American Christians are doers. What we discovered was that this wasn't about doing at all. It was all about relationships. People are, well, people, not projects. We were led to that place to develop relationships with one another. Anyone who has participated in a short-term mission/vision trip will tell you they received more than they gave, and that's the mystery of the ministry of presence.

FINDING OUR PLACE
IN THE STORY

1. "People have expressed profound gratitude to God for our showing up wherever we've gone. They felt loved and seen by him." Have you done something selfless and heard others give God praise and thanks? What did you notice?

2. "How could we celebrate in a way that expressed our gratitude to God for twenty-five years of married life and blessed someone else simultaneously?" Is there something you want to give God special recognition and thanks for? How can you include him?

3. "Zambia was out of this hemisphere and out of my comfort zone." Is God asking you to do something out of your comfort zone? (Don't worry; he doesn't ask many of us to go to Africa, but he may ask you to go across the street.)

4. "We discovered this wasn't about doing at all." How are you encouraged by knowing we don't need special abilities or qualifications to be used by God?

13

"Plenty Fish"

"For he and all his companions were astonished
at the catch of fish they had taken ..."

LUKE 5:9

In the Lozi language, Mwandi means "plenty fish," which should have been a clue about what would happen next.

Fish figure prominently in the biblical narrative. From creation, Jonah, and the calling of fishermen as the first disciples to the feeding of the five thousand in the Gospels. In John's Gospel,[41] the resurrected Jesus engineers a miraculous catch of 153 fish and cooks a fish breakfast. During the times of persecution by the Romans in the first centuries, the fish symbol (ichthys, the Greek word for fish) was used among Christians in hiding to display places for everyone to meet and worship. As early as the first century, Christians made an acrostic from this word: Iesous Christos Theou Yios Soter, i.e., Jesus Christ, Son of God, Savior.[42]

In a Dallas hotel room in 1996, I heard the call to "feed my sheep," and I assumed he meant to feed them spiritual food. I was about to learn there are many layers to God's plan and purpose for

---

41 John 21:1–14

42 Elesha Coffman, "What is the origin of the Christian fish symbol?" Christian History, August 8, 2008, https://www.christianitytoday.com/history/2008 /august/what-is-origin-of-christian-fish-symbol.html.

our lives. Much of Kingdom work isn't either-or. It is often both-and. Fish were about to become a significant focus in my life and in Rury Waddell's.

David Inman Memorial Fish Farm

At the end of that first "vision trip," Rury approached the team with the idea of starting a fish farm to raise tilapia. Food security is an ongoing struggle in Mwandi, and a fish farm could be a more consistent source of protein for the village. It would also create jobs for some of the unemployed men. Any profit from the sale of the fish would be used to offset the ongoing operating expense of the Orphan and Vulnerable Children Project (OVC).

The upper Zambezi River, where Mwandi is located, is home to seventy-three fish species. These species are threatened by unsustainable fishing practices, removing fry and fingerlings, which are needed to replenish stocks and as food for larger fish. Fish farming, or aquaculture, is increasingly used in developing nations (Majority World[43]) countries, but there were many challenges and hurdles to seeing a fish farm become a reality in Mwandi. I was looking for where God was inviting Sharon and me to join him in Africa, so I wondered if this could be it. But I knew absolutely nothing about aquaculture.

While in Africa, I created a blog about our daily activities and the ongoing struggles of the Lozi people. When I returned home from that first trip, a check was waiting for me from my friend Elaine Rudolph. She followed the blog and wanted to help the people she read about. Her accompanying note said, "Use where needed." There was no appeal for funds; the money just showed up.

---

43 Shahidul Alam, "Majority World: Challenging the West's Rhetoric of Democracy," *Amerasia Journal 34*, no. 1 (2008):87–98, http://dx.doi.org/10.17953/amer.34 .1.l3176027k4q614v5.

A sign from heaven? I called her and asked if she wanted to help start a fish farm. She was all in.

The second person to contribute was Dave Inman, a colleague and friend from Carroll Financial, where we both worked. Dave was an avid fisherman himself. He was excited about the potential of the fish farm and loved the idea. Tragically, Dave died unexpectedly soon after. As a tribute to him, many of his friends at Carroll contributed significantly financially to this endeavor, with the firm matching those gifts. Friends from church and Rotary International helped, too. We had enough funds to launch Rury's project in a few weeks. I never asked people to give, but when they heard or read the stories, something (or someone) stirred in them to want to help. God was on the move, and so was I ... back to Africa.

Now that we had the funds, there was much to do. Rury decided the farm would consist of ponds about a hundred yards from the Zambezi River. Water would be pumped from the river to the ponds. The first challenge was getting the pond to hold water, as the soil was mostly sand, so Rury purchased material from South Africa to create a liner. Sounds simple enough, but nothing is simple or accessible in the Majority World. Our collected funds would help finance the first pond liner and our tilapia fingerlings.[44]

The Bible reminds us that God's grace is sufficient for us, and his power is made perfect in our weakness (2 Corinthians 12:9). His grace was fully displayed in this endeavor. We needed his help in getting the liner delivered and installed and in getting the fingerlings. By a minor miracle, the liner arrived when we were in Mwandi, so we participated in the installation.

The liner was 150 x 21 feet and had to be cut in half, and then a seam had to be melted together to prevent leaking. We lined

---

44 "What are tilapia fingerlings?" Aquabest Seafood, accessed July 25, 2024, http://aquabestseafood.com/what-are-tilapia-fingerlings/.

the ends and sides of the liner with seventy-five-pound sandbags, which we dug, filled, and installed. I was so glad someone brought Aleve with them that day. Working with a black liner under the hot African sun was a primary concern, but we received another gift of grace. As we began to lay the liner into the pond, clouds rolled in and blocked the sun completely. Amazing grace! We worked hard and long, filling the fish pond with water by sundown. Now, all we needed was fish. How hard could that be?

The Legend of Chief Mickey Charlie

Rury knew of an established fish farm only a few hours' drive away, which was good news. They might be willing to sell us some tilapia fingerlings, but we didn't know how to contact them, and they were in another country. Namibia, not Zambia. Bad news. We also needed a way to transport the fish back to Mwandi and across the border, alive, without a supply of oxygen. Several fish puns would work here, but "a fish out of water" would be fine to describe how I felt. Rury was calm and relaxed as always, but once again, I was "in the deep end" and "in over my head." I did the only thing I knew to do: I got my camera and followed Rury.

When reading or studying the scriptures, I am always alerted to the stories that begin with "But God." We needed a "But God" in this story … big time. Faced with insurmountable odds, we loaded a three-hundred-gallon water tank onto a commercial-sized flatbed truck and headed to Likunganelo Fish Farm in Namibia. When my anxiety was beginning to subside, it was time to cross the border and go through customs. That's when I saw the guys with machine guns. Cue the nerves. Rury did all the talking; I just did what he did because I didn't understand anything. They might have spoken

English, but the accents sometimes perplexed me, and I couldn't understand.

But God (and Rury) guided us, and we were on our way into Namibia in search of the Likunganelo Fish Farm. We didn't have an address or GPS; we had Rury. He had a vague idea of where it was and didn't disappoint. Within an hour, we pulled into the farm, which was open and operating. (Thank God.) The men and women who managed the business seemed very willing to help us. I said, "seemed very willing," because I still couldn't follow the dialogue. All I could do was smile and take pictures.

At one juncture, they wanted to know who I was. "Mike Jette," I said. They made me spell it because they were struggling with the pronunciation. "Mickey," they said for Mike, pronouncing the once-silent "e" now as an "ey." That was the easy one. "Charlie," they said for Jette. That's me, Mickey Charlie.

We were informed that for them to sell us the fingerlings, we needed the permission of the government officials who oversaw the operation. We would have to travel back the way we came to Katima, incurring a significant delay and uncertain outcome. But God wasn't done helping us because the officials we needed to speak with arrived at the fish farm unexpectedly. After a brief conversation with Rury, they agreed to sell us all the fingerlings we could carry.

The fingerlings would have to be caught and then transferred into our tank. The workers caught the fingerlings in a net and sorted them on shore before tossing the keepers into our tank. This process took a long time, which meant our little fish struggled to stay alive in the poorly oxygenated water. Rury paid our new friends, shoved the receipt into his pocket, and off we went, fish jumping out of the tank, trying to escape. It would take at least two hours to return to Mwandi, and we still had to clear customs. Not good!

But God guided us through customs again, and no one looked in the water tank. The fish stopped jumping out, which we later learned was a bad sign. We made it the rest of the way home, and as we neared the fish pond, the truck got stuck in the sand from our cargo's weight. Another hour passed as Rury's farm crew maneuvered the tank to the pond and dumped it. It was dark by then, but we could see many dead fingerlings floating in the pond. No wonder they stopped jumping out. It was not our best moment.

The following day, when we went to investigate, it looked like the Dead Sea … with thousands of dead tilapia floating everywhere. To our amazement, we did see a few fish swimming around. It was deflating then, but God would soon multiply those into thousands. Tilapia fingerlings grow quickly and are prolific reproducers, and our tilapia would thrive in their new surroundings. Mwandi had a fish farm.

Rury reached into his pocket and showed me the receipt he was given at Likunganelo. He was laughing because the fish farm managers had made the receipt out to me. Perhaps because I was older, had gray hair, and walked around taking pictures looking like I was in charge, they thought Rury worked for me. The receipt was made out to "Chief Mickey Charlie."

Rury named it The David Inman Memorial Fish Farm to honor and acknowledge David's contribution and memorial gifts. A plaque with the name adorns that holy ground. In the next few months and subsequent years, we would witness a "But God Multiplication Miracle" as our tilapia numbered in the tens of thousands.

Feed My Sheep

Food security means knowing where your next meals are coming from—not just for today, but for the weeks, months, and years to come. It also means knowing the food will be nutritious enough to lead active and healthy lives and fuel children's futures. Most importantly, it means knowing God is our provider and source of everything we need.

Our interactions with the OVC and fish farm staff included Bible devotions and budgeting classes. Seeing what God was doing to help feed the people of Mwandi physically and spiritually was encouraging. We know our God can do more than we can ask or imagine. The David Inman Memorial Fish Farm is a testimony to this. Little did we know, however, that we were about to participate in another multiplication miracle. God is good at math. And why not? He created it.

FINDING OUR PLACE
IN THE STORY

1. God's plans and purposes for our lives have many layers. Much of Kingdom work isn't either-or. It is often both-and. How can we avoid "either-or" thinking and explore the multilayered nature of ministry?

2. "When reading or studying the scriptures, I am always alerted to the stories that begin with 'But God.'" What "But God" stories do you have?

3. "The following day, when we investigated, it looked like the Dead Sea … with thousands of dead tilapia floating everywhere." How can we better cope with obstacles and discouragement in our daily lives?

4. Food security is an ongoing struggle in many places throughout the Majority World. Ask God to show you where he wants to partner with you in loving your hungry neighbors. Take the first next step.

14

Multiplication Miracle

"Taking the five loaves and the two fish and looking up to heaven, he gave thanks and broke the loaves. Then he gave them to the disciples, and the disciples gave them to the people. They all ate and were satisfied, and the disciples picked up twelve basketfuls of broken pieces that were left over. The number of those who ate was about five thousand men, besides women and children."

MATTHEW 14:19–21

Food security, economic opportunity, and health are challenges to human flourishing in the Majority World. One tool that is helping to address each of these areas is the proliferation of micro-finance. This story is not about micro-finance, not really. It's an essential component, but this is about the miracle of multiplication, leftovers, and breadcrumbs. Like the miracle of the loaves and fishes, this story is about how God can multiply what is in our hands when we put them in his. We resembled the disciples in the Gospel story because we had no clue what God would do. We wanted to help, and we depended on him (through breadcrumbs) to guide us.

Micro-finance is a banking service provided to low-income individuals or groups who otherwise would have no other access to financial services through small or "micro" loans. In particular, we stumbled upon (via a breadcrumb) an emerging methodology called Village Savings and Loan Associations (VSLAs). When appropriately implemented, this program has profound implications for advancing human flourishing among the poorest of the poor.

A famous credit card commercial on TV asks, "What's in your wallet?"[45] During the burning bush discourse, God asked Moses, "What's that in your hand?"[46] Moses was holding a shepherd's staff. The Lord turned the staff into a snake and back into a staff again. That staff would have a critical recurring role in the Exodus story. Moses learned that little things in our hands become big things in his. We were about to see this for ourselves.

Another reason, I believe, that the Lord wanted me to write this book is so other "beggars" like me would see how he can use anyone, even a financial planner. He wants to partner with you and me in this great redemption story. The Lord is asking us the same question he asked Moses. When I first went to Zambia, I couldn't see how a financial planner could help. The thing in my hand was a planning background.

Our experience with VSLAs in the Global South is nothing short of mind-blowing. We depended on the Lord's leading because we knew nothing about micro-finance beyond being able to spell it. The road forward was paved with many unexpected twists and turns (more breadcrumbs).

Poverty 101: Helping Without Hurting

In my initial African experience, I could see how deficient I was in understanding poverty. God used the world of micro-finance as

---

45 Staff Writer, "What is 'What's in Your Wallet'?" Reference.com, updated August 4, 2015, https://www.reference.com/business-finance/s-wallet-19c2c b5d428be010.

46 Exodus 4:2–4

a conduit for my continuing education and understanding of the challenges of living in the Majority World.

On the various short-term mission trips we participated in over the years, a common denominator was to focus on a project we would do or teach. We were there to build, paint, train, or hand out gifts to help people less fortunate than ourselves. We intended to be a helpful blessing, and to some extent, I hope we were, but I fear we often did more harm than good.

Our poverty education was heavily influenced by *When Helping Hurts: How to Alleviate Poverty Without Hurting the Poor ... and Yourself.*[47] In their book, Steve Corbett and Brian Fikkert explain how some poverty relief efforts reinforce others' sense of powerlessness, especially when administered in a spirit of paternalism.

This came into focus after our first trip to Mwandi. Fiona Dixon-Thompson (later Fiona Waddell) launched the Mwandi OVC project in 1999 in partnership with one of the local churches there. She asked us to paint the new sewing center at the OVC as a short-term mission team. It was constructed with concrete blocks, which we found challenging to paint with brushes and rollers. It was hard work, and we were glad to do it. It never occurred to us that there might have been a better way to help. Most Zambian villages have a shortage of jobs and income, and Mwandi was no exception. The villagers often watched us work when we could have hired local men, trained, paid, and worked alongside them. We implemented this idea the next time we returned to Mwandi in 2009.

In their book, Corbett and Fikkert argue that all poverty's root causes can be categorized as a breakdown of four key relationships: with God, with others, with creation, and with ourselves. Every human being is poor in not experiencing these four relationships

---

47 Steve Corbett and Brian Fikkert, *When Helping Hurts* (Chicago, IL: Moody Publishers, 2014).

as God intended. Said another way, the gospel is the only path to escape all poverty because it is the only way to restore all four broken relationships.

In her book *Agents of Flourishing*, Amy Sherman wrote, "The Hebrew word shalom captures the notion of peace in these four relationships. Shalom signifies spiritual, psychological, social, and physical wholeness. And shalom is God's normative intention for us. Shalom is what we find in his original creation, and shalom is what will characterize the new heaven and new earth in his consummated kingdom. God designed us for flourishing."[48]

Corbett and Fikkert explain, "Our tendency is to define poverty in physical terms—the poor tend to describe it in psychological terms such as humiliation, shame, powerlessness, and isolation." I understood that if we were going to help others without hurting them or ourselves, we would need an approach that addressed the root causes and types of poverty, including the psychological.

Another lesson we learned about short-term missions was the need to understand our poverty. When equipped with the right mindset, we can always learn something from people who are different from us. I became keenly aware of my spiritual poverty as I witnessed the robust faith of some of the materially poor. We had much to learn from them.

In Matthew 16:26, Jesus said, "What good will it be for someone to gain the whole world, yet forfeit their soul? Or what can anyone give in exchange for their soul?" I began to see the danger of helping people lift themselves out of material poverty but leaving them in bondage to other expressions of poverty. Indeed, there is more to becoming a whole and healthy person than money and

---

48 Amy Sherman, *Agents of Flourishing: Pursuing Shalom in Every Corner of Society* (Lisle, IL: InterVarsity Press, 2022).

possessions. We need holistic approaches to poverty alleviation. We need to become agents of human flourishing.

God at Work

Fiona Waddell created several initiatives to help the Mwandi community, and she invited me to help them explore micro-finance options. She wondered if there was a way to use it as part of the OVC's sewing center program. The sewing center was built to help create the means to enable a person or a family to support themselves through their work. The loans could help start or keep a small business like sewing. The funds would be used to purchase fabrics and their machines.

My knowledge of the topic was rudimentary, but there was a financial component, so I hoped I would be more helpful than I was with fish farming. But where to begin? I trusted the Lord and relied on him to lead me. He didn't disappoint. He supplied one of many "breadcrumbs" through our dear friend Karen Lynip, a retired missionary to the Philippines.

When Karen heard I was interested in micro-finance, she introduced me to a book called *The Poor Will Be Glad: Joining the Revolution to Lift the World Out of Poverty* by Peter Greer and Phil Smith. Peter is the president and CEO of Hope International (Hope), a nonprofit organization focused on the Majority World, utilizing various micro-finance tools. Karen also introduced me to Peter, who "happened" to be her nephew (another breadcrumb). I contacted Peter, thinking Hope could bring micro-finance to Mwandi.

In our conversation, Peter explained that Mwandi lacked the population required and was too remote to consider a traditional micro-finance banking model. But he told me of a growing movement that could be useful to us: Village Savings and Loans Association (also known as savings groups) (a breadcrumb). In Corbett and Fikkert's book, I learned that the Chalmers Center organization was training others in a biblically based approach to VSLAs (breadcrumb).[49] In their model, people gather weekly to worship, study God's Word, pray, save money, and make loans. One strength of this approach is how it empowers the poor. VSLA groups are self-sustaining, as members do not rely on money from banks or donors. The members learn that their human and financial capital comes from their relationship with God and each other … not a well-meaning missionary or financial institution.

VSLAs

A VSLA is a self-selected group of people who pool small amounts of money into a communal fund from which members can borrow. The short-term loans from this fund are paid back with interest, causing the fund to grow.

After a complete cycle (one year), all or part of the total funds (including interest earnings) will be distributed to the individual members. The lump sums are usually based on a formula linked to the amount saved. This distribution provides a large amount of money each member can apply to their needs.

VSLA members can borrow with a minimum of fuss, access loans and insurance benefits approved by their peers, and obtain loans ranging from small change to several hundred dollars. Typical loans are usually between $10 and $50, which is far too small for formal banks or regular micro-finance institutions to consider. Members can receive insurance services that offset the effects of

---

49 "Restore," Chalmers.org, accessed July 25, 2024, https://chalmers.org/training /restore-savings/.

unforeseen disasters and set up funds for school fees, festivals, and other predictable annual events.

At the heart of the savings group's methodology is the reality that impoverished people can and do save. Another strength of the model is the focus on savings first—before loans. In the banking model, loans come first. Leading with savings helps establish a person as a credible loan risk.

Savings groups are informal, but that doesn't mean they are unorganized. In implementing the methodology, there are constitutions to write, officers to elect, recordkeepers to train, a lock box, and lots of transparency. These mechanisms are the program's greatest strengths and most significant obstacles. To do this right requires a lot of training at the start-up.

VSLA in Mwandi

At that time, Hope International was not utilizing the VSLA concept, but they did have a staff person, Mark, who had helped create VSLAs in … Zambia … in his free time (a breadcrumb). (Hope would, however, embrace it in future years.) Peter Greer introduced us, and Mark told me he used a biblical methodology in Zambia. These savings groups were church-sponsored, making group self-selection easier as villagers were already acquainted with one another and knew who could be trusted.

Mark couldn't go with us to Zambia, but he was willing to come to Charlotte from Lancaster, Pennsylvania, to train us so we could help train the first savings groups in Mwandi (another breadcrumb). He borrowed heavily from the work of the Chalmers Center and the Aga Kahn Foundation, which were leaders in the movement. I recruited seven others who volunteered to be trained.

Four of us would take the methodology to Mwandi in July of 2011: Eric deNeve, Steve Grey, Ben Johnson, and me.

Mark learned of a VSLA training course right after ours in Johannesburg, South Africa (breadcrumb). Our seven Charlotte trainees cobbled our resources and raised enough money to send Rury to Johannesburg to be trained. We knew this would be helpful because Rury would be in Mwandi to manage the program. We didn't realize at the time just how providential and pivotal this would be.

Before we could launch the program in Mwandi, we needed the approval of the local Mwandi leadership. That meant another trip to Africa to present the concept at a meeting with His Royal Highness Senior Chief Inyambo Yeta and the Mwandi Kuta in the spring of 2011. The meeting with the Kuta occurred outside, as we projected a VSLA video in English onto a sheet. We could tell that most of their leadership didn't understand what was being said, and at least one member fell asleep. But by God's grace and Rury's guidance, we obtained permission.

In July 2011, we returned to Mwandi to help train and launch the first VSLAs. It was exhilarating to see it all finally come together—we had two fully operational VSLAs!

VSLAs & Human Flourishing

How have VSLAs contributed to human flourishing among the poorest of the poor? I have visited many active VSLAs in Southern Africa and have heard the members share how VSLA has blessed and helped them. An excellent illustration of God's provision through VSLA is the story of Gertrude, who participated in one of the first groups in Mwandi. Gertrude is a widowed grandmother caring for nine grandchildren. Like many others, if her fragile and externally dependent income stream is interrupted, no bank officer is on speed dial to bail her out. The loss of income or an unexpected financial obligation often means going without the bare essentials like food, clothing, and education for her grandchildren, and it could even mean eviction from her two-room rented house.

The most dramatic result of the VSLA program is often in the participants' increased self-respect and social capital. Women, like Gertrude, make up 70 percent of the membership. VSLA groups are filling a financial and social gap that has been missing for years in most of central Africa. The collective empowerment of women that has developed due to the independence and security that VSLAs have brought them is as significant a transformation as the financial independence they now experience. For a widow like Gertrude, VSLA allowed her to be independent of loan sharks and church feeding programs. Gertrude directly relates to a local VSLA facilitator who assists her and other women in her community with accessing VSLA programs and the social empowerment that comes with it.

The transformation this simple methodology can create in communities is staggering, and the amount of money these groups will turn over this year is sizable. VSLA is one way the Church Universal is beginning to combat extreme poverty. This radically differs from traditional charity because it focuses on long-term, systemic change at the community level and employs lasting, local employment solutions, not short-term quick fixes. VSLA emphasizes the importance of church-and-community partnerships, and local champions like Gertrude are not external "saviors." VSLA is one way that the hope of the gospel is integrated into tangible acts of compassion that have long-term reach rather than simply providing handouts that keep the poor in a position of dependency. Through programs like VSLA, people like Gertrude can have financial stability in a volatile world.

Twelve Basketfuls of Leftover Breadcrumbs

Amy Sherman writes, "In God's world, multiplication is possible." Created in God's image, human beings are ingenious creators who can cooperatively bring out, develop, and multiply the world of possibilities that God made. As John Bolt puts it in *Economic Shalom*, "We were created for creative production … for using the manifold riches of creation to enhance human flourishing."[50]

We had hoped VSLA would multiply, but we could never conceive what God would do. Within a year from the time the first two VSLAs were launched, Rury was recruited by World Renew, the mission arm of the Reformed Church of North America. They hired him to be their Program Consultant for Zambia (big breadcrumb). When he told me this new position would require them to move from Mwandi, I feared all the progress would wither and vanish. I couldn't have been more wrong.

As Rury was established in his new position, he introduced VSLAs to World Renew in Southern Africa (Zambia, Malawi, and Mozambique). After witnessing their transformative impact in Zambia, he was asked to train his colleagues and World Renew's regional church partners in the methodology. Today, 5,749 small- and medium-sized enterprises and approximately 32,705 individuals participate in World Renew's VSLAs. In the last two quarters

---

50 Amy Sherman, *Agents of Flourishing: Pursuing Shalom in Every Corner of Society* (Lisle, IL: InterVarsity Press, 2022).

alone, $915,740 was saved, and 6,241 loans were created.[51] The methodology's success, reliability, and replicability mean that these numbers will continue to grow.

We followed the breadcrumb trail through many months and various interactions with Fiona Waddell, Karen Lynip, Peter Greer, Amy Sherman, Corbett and Fikkert, Mark, the Chalmers Center, the Aga Kahn Foundation, Rury Waddell, Chief Inyambo Yeta, the Mwandi Kuta, and finally, the staff at World Renew. From humble beginnings in Mwandi, we witnessed God's multiplicative prowess, in partnership with human beings, to enhance human flourishing among the poorest of the poor. After feeding more than five thousand people with two fish and five loaves, the disciples collected twelve basketfuls of breadcrumbs. Today, through VSLAs across the Global South, his VSLA breadcrumbs feed tens of thousands. Our time in Africa was for a season, and I am keenly aware of how privileged we were to see God work through us in this way.

I don't believe this story was about Africa or micro-finance. The multiplication miracle wasn't the end; it was the means to the end. This was about loving your neighbor. Sometimes, when we come to Jesus with a need, he says, "You give them something to eat."[52] Some folks were angry with me with every trip I made to Africa. They couldn't understand why we needed to go that far to love the poor, as they are everywhere. We don't have to go to Africa to love others. An act of love could be as simple as praying with someone sitting across from us who is hurting. We went because God asked us to. Period.

---

51 Ruairidh Waddell according to Beth DeGraff, "World Renew Announces Program Chief," Christian Reformed Church, January 3, 2024, https://www.crcna.org/news-and-events/news/world-renew-announces-program-chief.
52 Mark 6:37

As long as we are still alive, more opportunities remain. Mother Teresa captured the essence of the transformational power of love unleashed when we obey God: "Not all of us can do great things. But we can all do small things with great love."[53]

---

53 Ellen Mongan, "Small Things Done with Great Love," CatholicMom.com, January 3, 2017, https://www.catholicmom.com/articles/2017/01/03/small -things-done-great-love.

FINDING OUR PLACE
IN THE STORY

1. Imagine God is asking you, as he did to Moses, "What's that in your hand?"[54] How do you answer?

2. "Some poverty relief efforts reinforce others' sense of powerlessness, especially when administered in a spirit of paternalism." When have you seen this in your experience with helping others?

3. "There is more to becoming a whole and healthy person than money and possessions." Can you name all the things that make us whole and healthy?

4. How do VSLAs contribute to human flourishing?

5. Sometimes, when we come to Jesus with a need, he says, "You give them something to eat." Ask God to show you where he wants to partner with you in loving your struggling neighbors. Take the first next step.

---

54 Exodus 4:2

15

Treasure Discovered

"But store up for yourselves treasures in heaven, where moths and
vermin do not destroy, and where thieves do not break in and
steal. For where your treasure is, there your heart will be also."

MATTHEW 6:20–21

"The kingdom of heaven is like treasure hidden in a field.
When a man found it, he hid it again, and then in his joy
went and sold all he had and bought that field."

MATTHEW 13:44

When you read the word "treasure," I first want you to think of money and possessions. Treasure can be more than that, of course, but I want to discuss our stuff. In chapter 3, "Boom," I wrote that we are eternal beings in a temporal experience. A tension exists for us to live in the balance of temporal and eternal. Jesus was acutely aware of this and encouraged his followers to live in the present, ever mindful of eternity. When he talked about money or possessions, he encouraged us to share with others. God has many reasons for wanting us to become generous, and one of them is to show us how we can measure our progress in balancing the temporal and eternal. Another reason is that he wants us to know how our temporal giving will positively impact us in eternity.

In religious circles, we typically refer to giving as a tithe. In biblical terms, tithing can refer to giving a tenth, or 10 percent, of one's income or resources to support the work of the church or the religious community. One question often asked of me is, "How much is the tithe?" It is one way of asking how much one is required to give. Is it 10 percent? Do we tithe on our net income or the gross? I stopped trying to answer this many years ago because I honestly don't know, and I think it is the wrong question. To ask a better question requires a paradigm shift in our understanding of giving.

Jesus's teachings were unambiguous on what some have called "The Treasure Principle."[55] Jesus taught us that we could store up treasure in heaven for ourselves. He guaranteed it would be there for us, and his guarantee is better than the FDIC. The modern-day martyr and missionary Jim Elliott said something similar, "He is no fool who gives what he cannot keep to gain what he cannot lose."[56] Elliott wasn't talking about money; he was referring to laying down his life for Jesus, which is precisely what he did. On January 8, 1956, Jim Elliot, Nate Saint, Ed McCully, Peter Fleming, and Roger Youderian were speared to death on a sandbar in the Curaray River of Ecuador. They were trying to reach the Huaorani Indians for the first time in history with the gospel.

Elliott spoke about giving his life, but this principle also applies when we give away our money. If you knew, without a doubt, there was a way to convert dollars into eternal currency by giving it away, how much would you give? Think about it: forever is a long time. In a way, Jesus is showing us a better way to be self-centered ... by

---

55 Randy Alcorn, *The Treasure Principle: Unlocking the Secret of Joyful Giving* (Sisters, OR: Multnomah Books, 2005).

56 Elisabeth Elliot, *Shadow of the Almighty: The Life & Testament of Jim Elliot* (New York, NY: HarperCollins, 2009).

being generous in this life, he will reward us in the next. Forever. Jesus isn't anti-reward; he is pro-smart and anti-foolish.

When we give, we accumulate treasure in heaven, where we will live forever. Our earthly treasures will be left behind at our death, lost to us forever. We spend so much of our lives creating and protecting that wealth from thieves and other destructive forces. It can be exhausting and all-consuming. Someone asked the accountant of one of America's wealthiest men after his death, "How much did he leave?" The answer: "He left all of it."

From a biblical perspective, not being generous is incredibly foolish. Here's the principle: the wisest and safest thing to do with money is to give it to Jesus. This requires faith because you have to trust that God will meet your needs now and in eternity. Giving wealth away after your death does not require faith because it is no longer yours. Therefore, the eternal exchange rate for "dead dollars" is zero.

A Giving Journey

First, three disclaimers: 1) God doesn't need anything from me or you. The Bible teaches that God owns everything, and because everything in the heavens and earth belongs to him, he can take what he wants at any time. 2) Jesus reserved his highest praise for giving to the poor widow who put in two tiny copper coins, all she had to live on.[57] When we reach that level of faith, we will be in excellent company, but until then, we are all on a journey. 3) Our shared journey takes place over many years and is far from over. It's a long, ongoing process of discovery.

A friend once told me, "You can't take people places you've never been to." In generosity terms, this means you can't help people

---

57 Luke 21:1–4

understand giving unless you're on that path yourself. Spoiler alert! As you read about our experience, don't be surprised when God reveals himself to be incredibly generous, not Sharon and me.

We have grown in our giving as our understanding of generosity matured. In the beginning, we gave without thinking and without a plan. As the offering plate passed, we put a few bucks in, which many people were doing. I call this "I'm no worse than anybody else" giving. When the pastor would preach a "stewardship" sermon every fall, we'd squirm a little and feel guilty—this feeling quickly passed before the following Sunday. Stewardship has a broader meaning, but religious types have made it about giving to their church. It is sometimes synonymous with tithing. Tithing would be our next giving destination.

As we grew spiritually, our perspective about money and giving was evolving. Gradually, we stretched ourselves and began tithing on our net income—out of obligation. We were surprised by how smoothly that transition went, so our next step was to tithe on our gross earnings. According to Barna, only 5 percent of American Christians tithe.[58] I'm not sure why that number is so low, but I wonder if the cultural influence and emphasis on consumerism and accumulation are part of the explanation. In a parable, Jesus called this "building bigger barns." The punch line of the parable began with, "You fool!" And ended with, "This very night, your life will be demanded from you. Then who will get what you have prepared for yourself?"[59]

The next stop on our giving journey was tithing 10 percent of our gross to our church and giving above that to other ministries

---

58 "New Study Shows Trends in Tithing and Donating," Barna, April 14, 2008, https://www.barna.com/research/new-study-shows-trends-in-tithing-and -donating/.
59 Luke 12:16–21

unrelated to our church. Every time we stretched our faith by giving more, we were amazed that, even though we sacrificed some of our lifestyle, there was always enough money to cover our expenses and save a little. In Malachi 3:10, God gives Israel an atypical invitation and mind-bending promise: "'Bring the whole tithe into the storehouse, that there may be food in my house. Test me in this,' says the Lord Almighty, 'and see if I will not throw open the floodgates of heaven and pour out so much blessing that there will not be room enough to store it.'" This is the only place in the Bible that I am aware of where God invites us to test him.

We adopted the tithing concept as a place to start, not a finish line. Jesus said, "Give, and it will be given to you. A good measure, pressed down, shaken together and running over, will be poured into your lap. For with the measure you use, it will be measured to you."[60] Some religious professionals have twisted this into a prosperity gospel. We've all heard televangelists who appeal for funding and promise blessings in this life. For my cynical friends, this manipulation of the truth is a major stumbling block to growing in generosity.

Sharon and I saw it as an invitation to follow Jesus and get to know and trust him more. We had already won the "life lottery" when he rescued and adopted us into his family. Our giving journey was a way to explore the riches of his grace. God has chosen to bestow upon us his blessings based on his grace toward us, not on our obedience or faithfulness to the law. God's blessings are showered upon our lives not because we merit or deserve them but because God loves us, and we can't help that. I am so thankful for it. God is constantly overwhelming us with his grace and love.

By the end of 2006, we felt the Lord was leading us to greater faith in giving. We knew that we had reached a plateau or comfort

60 Luke 6:38

level in our giving and that it had been years since we had given at a level that would require us to experience increased faith in God. On January 1, 2007, Sharon and I prayed and promised God we would step out in faith and double our giving. Our tithe to our church was going to double from 10 percent to 20 percent, and our gifts to other ministries would double from previous levels.

I don't mind telling you that we had some anxiety about our commitment. We had resolved to do whatever it would take to fulfill our pledge. Years earlier, we had reduced our lifestyle spending to create more margin in our budget, but this was no slight stretch. We both were compensated on fees and commissions, so we never knew what we would earn in any given year.

During the first few months of 2007, we succeeded in funding our ongoing budget items, even as we tithed 20 percent of our gross income. We were off to a good start, but we had yet to determine where the funds for other gifts would come from other than our savings. Then, in May of 2007, something unexpected happened. Larry Carroll, the owner of our financial planning firm, asked me for help with one of his clients. We had no prior agreement on my remuneration, and we both thought working on this would be a waste of time. We were wrong.

While helping him, we closed the most significant deal our firm has ever done. Sharon and I tithed on our portion of the windfall and fulfilled our commitment to the other gifts. The Bible says, "Each of you should give what you have decided in your heart to give, not reluctantly or under compulsion, for God loves a cheerful giver."[61] We loved writing those checks to our church and ministries and felt God's presence and pleasure. Don't overlook the first part of that verse … "give what you have decided in your heart to give."

---

61 2 Corinthians 9:7

We have developed a repeatable practice for our annual financial gifts. At the end of each year, we prayerfully discern what our giving for the coming year will be, resolving in advance what we should give, could give, and would give. The process is always part faith and part educated guess. We like to be intentional, knowing our giving would be inconsistent and sloppy without a plan. It has worked well for us. But we also want to be spontaneous, and we've discovered other fun ways to be generous.

We are creative at giving away our cars. We helped people who couldn't afford a reliable car by selling them one of ours. Or at least that is what we wanted them to believe. We put each monthly payment into a separate savings account without telling them, and when they had finished making the payments, we gave the money back to them. They had a paid-for car and a nice emergency fund in the bank. It is a beautiful way to help someone—without hurting them.

As part of our Africa experience, Sharon and I helped put two young men through high school and college. We knew these boys personally, spent time with them, and saw them progress in their studies, which was a blessing and a privilege. We continue to stay in touch and encourage them because life isn't easy there, even with an education. They are important to us. This kind of giving is fun because we see how people's lives are improved.

Every day during our prayer time, we thank God for many blessings, including his provision. We thank him for giving us more than we need so we can share with others. We are excited to learn what God did with our gifts and how he blessed them and multiplied them for his glory. Our minds cannot possibly conceive of all he has done and is doing because of this partnership, but all will be revealed one day. Can't wait!

Our Treasure

In my spoiler alert at the beginning of the chapter, I wanted you to know that the story's hero is God because he is the ultimate standard for generosity. Tim Keller, in *The Prodigal God*, helpfully reminds us of the definition of prodigal: "recklessly extravagant, having spent everything."[62] God best fits a definition of prodigal because he is recklessly extravagant with his grace and spends everything pursuing his created people: "He who did not spare his own Son, but gave him up for us all—how will he not also, along with him, graciously give us all things?"[63] Based on the parable we call the prodigal son,[64] Keller invites us to consider that the younger and the older brother suffer from the same motive; they are primarily interested in what they can get from their father. I think Keller hoped we would see ourselves in the parable. Do we resemble the reckless rebellion of the younger son in the story or the dutiful older brother who sins by obeying the rules for the wrong reasons?

The father in the story reveals the humanly incomprehensible love that God our Father has for each of us and his earnest desire to forgive us and have a relationship with us. Our prodigal God—one whose lavish, extravagant, luxuriant love for us can only amaze us and give us great solace and comfort.

He is the treasure.

---

62 Timothy Keller, *The Prodigal God: Recovering the Heart of the Christian Faith* (Westminster, London: Penguin Books, 2008).
63 Romans 8:32
64 Luke 15:11–32

FINDING OUR PLACE
IN THE STORY

1. From a biblical perspective, why would giving our money to Jesus be the wisest and safest thing to do?

2. What reasons would God have for wanting us to become generous? Does he need us to? Is he worried?

3. "In the beginning, we gave without thinking and without a plan." What advantages can you see to having a giving plan?

4. In the parable of the prodigal son, what motivated the younger and older brothers to behave the way they did?

16

Relationships Are Forever

"But about the resurrection of the dead—have you not read what
God said to you, 'I am the God of Abraham, the God of Isaac, and
the God of Jacob'? He is not the God of the dead but of the living."
When the crowds heard this, they were astonished at his teaching."

MATTHEW 22:31–33

I had the privilege of spending time with my friend Eric deNeve a few days before he died. He had been ill for a long time and knew he was dying. In a moment when he could communicate, we discussed what was on the other side of death. Eric was an excellent architect, and I told him I hoped Jesus had some building projects lined up. Jokingly, I asked him to put in a good word for me when he got there. He managed to smile and promised to meet me at heaven's entrance on the day of my arrival.

The religious professionals of Jesus's time were often trying to trick or trap him with probing but insincere questions. In Matthew's Gospel, Jesus responds to a ridiculous hypothetical question about marriage at the resurrection. What I love about his answer is how it supports the teaching that we are eternal beings. God didn't say, "I was the God of Abraham, Isaac, and Jacob." He said, "I am."[65] They are all still very much alive. Because death is

---

65 Matthew 22:23–33

transitory, we can look forward to continuing relationships we value in the next life and creating countless new ones.

The Bible says, "Now faith is confidence in what we hope for and assurance about what we do not see."[66] One of the great hopes of the resurrection for followers of Jesus is the people we will reunite with when it's our turn to cross over. Reunions of all types have become more frequent for us these days. We find them very meaningful because these people are in our lives for a reason, and even if our paths don't cross again during this life, we will be together for eternity. Death is not the end but a door or path to what is next.

Love Shows Up

When our families were younger, the Jette clan often gathered for Christmas. Our children loved getting together with their cousins and became adept at taking funny shots at their grandparents and uncles. No one was immune, and nothing was sacred. Our parents hosted us in their small Florida home, and we all took turns in our homes. Our Christmas reunions were loud and full of laughter, with Christmas Eve charades being the most raucous. I still chuckle when I remember Dad acting out the words and titles he was trying to get us to say. His style was … unusual … but always memorable. One Thanksgiving, for their fiftieth wedding anniversary, Mom and Dad rented a beach home near Charleston, South Carolina, big enough for all of us. It might be the best thing we ever did as a family. These family reunions were a great model for other future family gatherings.

We've had a few mini family reunions. Sharon's and my parents are dead now, and our siblings are spread out around the country.

---

66 Hebrews 11:1

Their children have children, and getting everyone together is hard. We've discovered that doing multiple mini-reunions is a way to stay in touch with almost everyone ... especially post-COVID. We have been blessed to have good relationships with our siblings, nieces, and nephews. Sometimes, when parents die, family connections unravel, but both of ours have not. This is a direct result of everyone intentionally prioritizing family as best as possible.

We have made many great memories and recognize that these relationships can be eternal. Our Friday prayers are for our birth families, and we always include our desire to all be reunited in the Kingdom to come. We imagine everyone we love around the table at the wedding banquet described in Revelation 19 for Jesus and his bride, the church.

I've reunited with old college and high school friends in the last few years. People love or hate these things, and I am firmly in the "love them" camp. Recently, I learned of a small group of old college friends gathering for lunch. We had had some great times, and I had not seen or talked to some of these guys for over forty years. I invited myself to join them—in Milwaukee. I bought a same-day, round-trip plane ticket to Chicago, rented a car, drove to Milwaukee, and showed up thirty minutes early for lunch. Seeing these guys again was a blast. They told many stories of activities we did together, but I did not remember some of them. I could tell from what they said that I was there, but the details eluded me. After lunch, I drove back to Chicago and took the last plane to Charlotte. I was in bed by midnight. The next day, I told Sharon about the stories the guys shared and all the fun we had back then, but I was sorry I seemed to have missed most of it.

I have attended most of my high school reunions. The school no longer exists, but many of the friendships forged back then still do, as do a few of my grade school and old neighborhood friendships.

Whenever I return to Buffalo or Milwaukee, which isn't often, I connect with as many people as possible. I am blessed by these relationships and the bonds formed from these shared past experiences. They are a gift, and I value and appreciate them all. We will have all eternity to build on what we had together in our short time here.

Relationships, like cars, require maintenance—some more than others. Good relational maintenance comes through intentionality and planning. We make time for the activities and people that are important to us; love is spelled T I M E. I get strange looks when I tell people about my lunch in Milwaukee. I can tell you who *didn't* think it was weird—my college friends. We were all blessed. No one always gets it right regarding relationships, but it is good when we do.

The number of birthdays, graduations, weddings, anniversaries, and funerals you regularly attend depends on your life season. We are frequently in funeral mode these days. We missed more of these significant life events than we should have. It's hard because our friends and family are spread out nationwide, which adds cost and complexity. We're getting better at discerning when to say yes. We are also having some success in creating our own shared experiences.

We've invited friends and family to share beach homes with us, and recently, we created a special eightieth birthday treat for Sharon's brother Rex that involved hiring a personal chef to cook a fabulous meal. Smaller activities can be just as meaningful. A phone call, a card, a note, or a text at the right time are powerful ways to let others know they are important to us.

One of the more unusual smaller activities I've done is to send out Christmas cards in July. Obviously, the Hallmark channel picked up the "Christmas in July" idea and has run with it. I was an "influencer" long before anyone knew that was a thing. I send cards to people I think might be able to use a little Christmas cheer, and because everyone sends cards in December, why not send them a bit early? In this way, our cards stand out, and I design them. This has turned into a tradition that started by accident.

In the late 1990s, our friend Loonis McGlohon was very ill battling cancer. Loonis was a talented musician with a beautiful sense of humor. I would occasionally send him a personal note or card to let him know we were praying for him and his wife, Nan. One year in July, I used an old Christmas card to write him a note, as it was the only card I had on hand. Loonis thought that was hilarious, so I kept sending him a Christmas card each July. One year, I missed sending him one, and he told me how much he looked forward to them each year. After that, I always sent a card in July and decided to expand the list. Loonis passed away in 2002, but I kept sending cards to Nan and others. Nan is gone, too, but the tradition continues as I send cards to all those on my expanded list.

Every time we show up in the lives of others, it sends a beautiful message. It is reminiscent of the gospel story because that is what God did. He became one of us, took on human flesh, and entered our broken mess not to condemn us but to rescue us. That's what love does. Love shows up.

And because relationships are forever, we know our family and friends, like Eric, who loved Jesus, will show up for us when it's our turn to cross over. It's fun to think about everything we'll have to catch up on and discuss.

FINDING OUR PLACE
IN THE STORY

1. "Death is not the end but a door or path to what is next." Who are you looking forward to seeing again in eternity?

2. "Relationships, like cars, require maintenance—some more than others." What can we do to stay meaningfully connected to those we care about?

3. "Sometimes, when parents die, family connections unravel." Family dynamics can be challenging even when parents are alive. How can we be connectors and peacemakers in our families?

4. "Every time we show up in the lives of others, it sends a beautiful message. That's what love does. Love shows up." Who did you think of or who came to mind when you read this? What will you do about it?

17

Work Is Sacred

"So God created mankind in his own image, in the image of God
he created them; male and female he created them. God blessed
them and said to them, "Be fruitful and increase in number; fill the
earth and subdue it. Rule over the fish in the sea and the birds in
the sky and over every living creature that moves on the ground."

"… The Lord God took the man and put him in the
Garden of Eden to work it and take care of it."

GENESIS 1:27–28; 2:15

Work is not everyone's favorite four-letter word. A common Christian misconception is the belief that work results from Adam and Eve's failure (aka the fall). It was what I believed when I started my working life as a teenager and for many years after. Work felt like punishment and had to be endured until retirement … better known as a permanent vacation. One churched friend defined work as "trading hours for dollars." Unfortunately, this remains a prominent paradigm for many, and the Christian church shares much of the blame.

Genesis 1 and 2 reveal how work existed before Adam and Eve's fall from grace and was always a part of God's plan for us. His nature encompasses unfathomable creativity, and because we are God's image bearers, work is our opportunity to express our God-given creative ability and talents. In these chapters, we find the "Cultural Mandate," meaning we participate with the Creator in making and shaping culture with the best of heaven—beauty, goodness, and truth. All work can be pregnant with purpose and beauty when performed in partnership with God and for his glory. Our daily work is an act of worship with the God who created, called, and equipped us to do it ... no matter what kind of work it is.

"Vocation" is from the Latin "vocatio," meaning a call or summons.[67] Gene Edward Veith wrote, "The doctrine of vocation is one of the greatest—though strangely neglected and forgotten—teachings of the Reformation. Contrary to the common assumption, it is much more than a theology of work. Vocation has to do with God's providence, how he governs and cares for his creation by working through human beings."[68] All work is meant to be sacred.

Forrest Gump said, "I am not a smart man," and if you read this far, you know Forrest and I have much in common.[69] At the risk of sounding like a simpleton, since we spend most of our adult daylight hours at work, why not purposefully fill those hours now and for eternity? Is that possible? Yes, our work can and should be much more than trading hours for dollars. It should be considered our vocation, and all life should be lived *Coram Deo*, especially our work.

---

67 "Vocation," Wikipedia, last edited June 22, 2024, https://en.wikipedia.org/wiki/Vocation.

68 Gene Edward Veith, "The Doctrine of Vocation," The Gospel Coalition, accessed July 25, 2024, https://www.thegospelcoalition.org/essay/the-doctrine-of-vocation/.

69 *Forrest Gump*, directed by Robert Zemeckis (Paramount Pictures, 1994).

Integrity

Coram Deo (pronounced CORE-um DAY-oh) is a Latin phrase that means "before the face of God." To live Coram Deo is to live one's life in the presence of God, under the authority of God, and to the glory of God.[70] To live in the presence of God is to understand that whatever we are doing and wherever we are doing it, we are acting under the gaze of God. I cannot think of anything more inspiring and hopeful to build a life on ... much less a business or a ministry.

God's intention for humanity before creation was to live with integrity. Dictionaries define integrity as the quality or state of being complete or undivided.[71] The fall resulted in the loss of unity or integrity by or as if by breaking into parts or disintegrating. The evidence of our disintegrated lives is found in how contemporary Christians compartmentalize them.

We live in a "spiritual world" when involved in church, Bible study, or prayer. Most of the time, particularly in our vocational lives, we live in the "secular world." Often, Christians speak about leaving their secular jobs to enter "full-time Christian ministry." They pursue vocations in church, other nonprofit Christian organizations, or international missions. From this perspective, Christians who are not in full-time Christian service and are working in the secular world are second-class citizens. Sadly, we operate according to the worldview of the culture. The result is that God is no longer honored as Lord of all, and the influence of Christians with a biblical worldview is removed from the marketplace. The

70 "What is Coram Deo?" livingandlearningcoramdeo.com, accessed July 25, 2024, https://livingandlearningcoramdeo.com/what-is-coram-deo/.

71 "integrity," *U.S. Dictionary*, updated July 1, 2024, https://usdictionary.com /definitions/integrity/.

goal for every follower of Jesus is to live a life of integrity, to live Coram Deo.

To live through this biblical lens means rejecting the false dichotomy of the sacred versus the secular. One of the most inspiring aspects of Coram Deo is how it dismantles the myth of the secular-sacred divide. Bob Goff captured the simple truth of this reality when he said, "Don't call it ministry; call it Thursday."[72] To live Coram Deo in our time is a lot like swimming upstream against the cultural currents. It is not an easy path, and it's often lonely and costly. Ultimately, you must live with a compelling vision for eternity and the Kingdom of God. To those swept along by the culture, you will look foolish. To aid me with this challenge, I found it helpful to create a Kingdom-minded "scorecard" to guide, direct, and encourage me in my vocation.

Scorecards

I'm using the term "scorecard" to describe how a particular worldview tells us what to value. The world has created a secular scorecard for us. They offered me one that included a busy calendar, a successful business, a comfortable retirement, a lovely home, nice cars, and travel to desirable destinations. The local church has created a sacred scorecard for us, too. They offered me one that included an elder's position, Sunday church attendance, leading Bible studies, and tithing. On the surface, these aren't necessarily good or bad things. Most churched folks will tell you this is how we were taught to organize our lives. It's become an adopted extension of the separation of church and state. We've been taught to

---

72 Bob Goff according to Quotable Quote, "We don't need to call everything we do 'ministry' anymore ...," Goodreads.com, accessed July 25, 2024, https://www.goodreads.com/quotes/9719659-we-don-t-need-to-call -everything-we-do-ministry-anymore.

live life through different silos. You don't mix religion with work and work with religion. It's the opposite of Coram Deo, and it isn't biblical. Most Christians today have never been taught the Cultural Mandate from Genesis 1:27–28.

In a biblical worldview, there is only one scorecard, and it is all about God's purpose for our lives. It includes all the things we think of as sacred and secular. The scorekeeping I'm referring to is about developing a personal set of metrics to help us determine if our lives align correctly with his will and our calling. These metrics invite us to think broadly and deeply about a life of intentionality and purpose. Early into my planning career, I began developing a scorecard to help me define and measure the most meaningful metrics that combined the best of the sacred and the secular.

The planning culture provided metrics defining success by capturing assets under management (AUM) and fee revenue. AUM and fee revenue are important measures and good ways to allocate resources and reward outstanding performance. They are proven motivators that enable people to enjoy a rewarding career and lifestyle. They are foundational to building a business that can grow and thrive. They have limitations, however, in helping to capture more holistic goals. I created a set of metrics to capture the activity I believed would glorify God and help make me a loving, trusted, and influential advisor. These metrics are designed to ensure I put a client's needs above my own and serve to accomplish their financial goals. Above all else, my goal for every prospect and client is for them to feel well-served, loved, and blessed.

Creating your scorecard is simple, but it isn't easy. The process is the same regardless of the vocation. It applies to the person who stays home to care for the children and the rocket scientist. No two scorecards are identical because we are all unique. I began by asking what makes a client or prospect appointment good and godly at the same time. I wondered how to make the person sitting across from me more welcome and comfortable. How can I communicate that I don't need or want anything "from" them but am wholly and only "for" them? How can I bless others in my context? How can I contribute to the human flourishing of others? Every person and context is different, but there are aspects we can measure and do repeatedly to shape our behavior and focus. For those gifted in building a business, don't overlook how you influence the flourishing of your employees.

Each year on my work anniversary, I send the head of our firm, Larry Carroll, a thank-you letter or card, acknowledging how he has blessed me and many others. I remind him that what he initiated has positively influenced countless lives. The firm offered an excellent benefits package and a non-toxic workplace where everyone had the opportunity to do great work. Contributing to the flourishing of others through business is a high calling. This approach can also be financially rewarding. Building a vocation that combines the best of the sacred and the secular is *good* business.

One of my best learnings from twenty years as a Rotarian was, "He who serves best profits most." In 1911, "He Profits Most Who Serves Best" was approved as the Rotary motto. It was adapted from a speech by Rotarian Arthur Frederick Sheldon to the first convention held in Chicago the previous year. Sheldon declared that "Only the science of right conduct toward others pays. Business is the science of human services. He profits most who serves his fellows best."[73] It is as accurate today as it was in 1911. In addition to Rotary International, my thinking was influenced

---

73 John Price, "Rotary's official mottoes – Did You Know?" Rotary Club of Boise East, accessed July 25, 2024, https://portal.clubrunner.ca/6042/stories /rotary%E2%80%99s-official-mottoes-did-you-know.

by a movement of like-minded financial advisors that emerged nationwide called Kingdom Advisors (KA).[74]

Kingdom Advisors

Sir Isaac Newton is credited with saying, "If I have seen further, it is by standing on the shoulders of giants."[75] In the realm of financial planning from a biblical perspective, those giants are Larry Burkett, Ron Blue, Terry Parker, and Howard Dayton. Color me eternally grateful for these men and the organizations they founded, led, and greatly influenced.

In 1997, Larry Burkett, cofounder of Crown Financial Ministries, brought together sixteen friends and fellow professionals committed to biblically wise financial advice to form the Christian Financial Planning Institute (CFPI). In 2003, these men and women asked Ron Blue, founder of Blue Trust, to help them advance their vision by creating a new organization to catalyze the Christian financial professional community. Originally known as the Christian Financial Professionals Network (CFPN), the organization began to grow and thrive under Ron Blue's leadership. In 2007, it was renamed Kingdom Advisors.

Around that same time, my friend John Putnam and I introduced the first Kingdom Advisors (KA) Study Groups in the greater Charlotte region. The KA study groups, conferences, and resources combined to shape our thinking, influence our business practices, and create a close community of colleagues who were once competitors. We continue to be active in KA and count the

---

74 Kingdom Advisors (homepage), accessed July 25, 2024, https://kingdom advisors.com.

75 Roger Billings, " … another of my favorite quotes," Acellus, science.edu, November 20, 2018, https://www.science.edu/acellus/2018/11/newton -seeing-further/.

other members among our best friends and colleagues. We are helping one another shape businesses that honor God while disseminating biblically wise financial advice.

Only some vocations have a Kingdom Advisors-like organization to learn from and contribute to. John and I would have created our local study groups if KA had not come along. I have started many small groups organized around different topics because they would be impactful and helpful. It's not difficult, and it is smart. Please don't wait for someone else to do it. If your soul hungers for this kind of community, you can create it. Do what we did. Combine forces and invite others to join over a meal or a cup of coffee. You will love it, and they will be blessed.

Work Is Worship

Along with trading hours for dollars, another misconception is that the purpose of work is to provide for our families. In Genesis 22, God reveals himself as Jehovah Jireh—the God who provides. In the story, Abraham, in obedience, prepares to sacrifice Isaac on the mountain God showed him. At the last second, an angel of the Lord stops him and provides a substitute for Abraham to offer instead of his only son. Abraham called that place Jehovah Jireh, meaning, "The Lord will provide." Work is often the pathway of God's provision, but he is the source. Working with the wrong motives is unavoidable in a culture that emphasizes the individual as central to all life. It's not about us; it's about God. This is why work, at its heart, is worship, and all of life is sacred.

Worship is challenging to define, but I am using the word in the sense of worship as a form of love—a type of deep devotion. When I created a scorecard for my work, I wanted to integrate Jesus into the activity that consumed most of my day and week. It was intended to be an act of love and devotion, not a striving to provide for my family. Living with this kind of integrity helped me excel in my vocation, empowered by the right motives and depending on Jehovah Jireh for our provision. Our best work is worship, and it is sacred.

Reading the Gospels makes it easy to see yourself transported into the story and imagine being present. You never see Jesus striving or worried. He is homeless, and while he lacks many physical comforts, he does not lack contentment. He has faith in the Father to provide for all his needs. He teaches us the same thing near the end of the Sermon on the Mount. "So do not worry, saying, 'What shall we eat?' or 'What shall we drink?' or 'What shall we wear?' For the pagans run after all these things, and your heavenly Father knows that you need them. But seek first his kingdom and his righteousness, and all these things will be given to you as well."[76] Our job, our work, is to seek first the Kingdom and leave the rest to him. A Coram Deo mindset and a good scorecard can help you do that.

Pastor and author John Piper said, "Here is a vocation that will bring you more satisfaction than if you became a millionaire ten times over—Develop the extraordinary skill for detecting the burdens of others and devote yourself daily to making them lighter."[77] That sounds a lot like the Jesus of the Gospels. Follow him.

---

76 Matthew 6:31–33
77 John Piper, "The Law of Christ," desiringGod.org, August 14, 1983, https://www.desiringgod.org/messages/the-law-of-christ.

FINDING OUR PLACE
IN THE STORY

1. "Work felt like punishment and had to be endured until retirement ... better known as a permanent vacation. One churched friend defined work as 'trading hours for dollars.'" How would you define work and retirement?

2. Coram Deo means "Before the face of God."[78] How would knowing you are working under the gaze of God influence your work? Or if you are a student, how would it influence your schoolwork?

3. Bob Goff said, "Don't call it ministry; call it Thursday."[79] What do you think Bob meant by that?

4. What metrics would be on your scorecard if it included both the sacred and the secular and made others feel well-served, loved, and blessed? How can you contribute to the human flourishing of others?

---

78 "What is Coram Deo?" livingandlearningcoramdeo.com, accessed July 25, 2024, https://livingandlearningcoramdeo.com/what-is-coram-deo/.
79 Bob Goff according to Quotable Quote, "We don't need to call everything we do 'ministry' anymore ...," Goodreads.com, accessed July 25, 2024, https://www.goodreads.com/quotes/9719659-we-don-t-need-to-call-everything-we-do-ministry-anymore.

18

Office Chaplain

*"Now that I, your Lord and Teacher, have washed your feet,
you also should wash one another's feet."*

JOHN 13:14

We don't need permission or an official title to make it our aim to find creative and even whimsical ways to be a feet washer. As followers of Jesus, it's in our DNA. I'm not a professional chaplain, and I've never been trained to perform those duties. Because all of life is sacred, I continually seek ways to love and bless others, especially those I work with and see five days a week.

Jesus was showing us what it looked like to love one another. To wash the feet of the guests at a feast was the office of a slave. The disciples of the rabbis were supposed to provide their master's personal service, but when Jesus washed his disciples' feet, he was breaking old norms. One of the beautiful facets of Jesus was his intimacy with God, which brought him nearer than ever to people instead of separating him from them. As a follower of Jesus, I look for ways to show God's love to my colleagues, clients, and product vendors in the spirit of feet washing.

When I joined Carroll Financial in December 2000, it was a twelve-month experiment or trial. I helped our firm's founder and president, Larry Carroll, recruit and train other independent advisors, and when I wasn't doing that, I was free to try to build my planning practice. Those twelve months have turned into twenty-four years and counting.

While Larry and I worked together, he said he thought of me as the office chaplain. This unofficial chaplaincy most likely began when I started a Bible study in the firm, like the one I attended hosted by Larry's friend Richard McCoy. Richard had invited Ken Schultz from Search Ministries to lead us through their Foundations curriculum. Ken was skilled in asking great questions that made complex faith ideas digestible, and he was a master in small-group dynamics. Ken became a valued mentor, brother in Jesus, and dear friend for life. He encouraged me when I started a Foundations study at Carroll.

The goal was to create a safe place for colleagues and others to learn about Jesus and the foundational truths of the Christian faith. Sometimes, a church is the last place you feel safe to get your questions answered. I invited my coworkers and a few friends from outside the company. We cobbled together a small group that continued to meet for many years.

The chaplaincy experience grew and matured through a prayer ministry. Over time, I learned the names of everyone's families, including spouses, children, and grandchildren. When possible, I extended an invitation to share any prayer requests. My door was always open if someone wanted to pray or talk. A wonderful, dearly departed saint, Cleo "Pete" Mead, told us, "A burden shared is a burden halved." She was right; after sharing a burden, we do feel lighter. Many felt safe and welcome, took me up on my offer, and continued doing so.

Our firm experienced three unexpected employee deaths over twelve months. This was unprecedented and shocking for a firm of less than fifty employees. We were able to grieve the loss and celebrate the lives of our colleagues through thoughtful all-employee memorials in our office. It was a very difficult season, and we continue to remember them on the anniversary of their passing. It honors their memory and communicates how we value one another as human beings.

Around this time, I began going on short-term mission trips to Zambia. In the office breakroom, I'd list items the people in Zambia could use, and my coworkers would enthusiastically participate with contributions. One of the best things we did was to raise enough money to start a tilapia fish farm (see chapter 13) in memory of David Inman, one of those three who died unexpectedly.

Larry and I worked closely together because of my recruiting and training responsibilities for the firm. I was a "fly on the wall" during hundreds of his conversations with prospective advisors, giving me insight and wisdom concerning all facets of our industry. I often told confidants it felt like I received an informal master's degree. In truth, what I learned was more valuable than a diploma and made me a better advisor. Larry and I have a close and unique relationship that we value highly and are grateful for. His wife, Vivian, even joined a small group of us on one of those trips I made to Zambia.

Feet washing can take many different forms in different circumstances and seasons. Through these years, it has been my privilege to play a pastoral role with numerous colleagues and clients in times of death, divorce, poor health, and financial upheaval. Many have said I was one of their first calls in times of distress. What an amazing and sacred privilege.

When we partner with God, he will surprise us. His love, mercy, grace, and creativity have no limits. God is in the outcome business. We are in the obedience business. He may not ask you to become an office chaplain, but he does have something for you to do wherever you are. When we follow him, we don't see the physical Jesus … we see the transformation only possible through him. He still turns water into wine.

FINDING OUR PLACE
IN THE STORY

1. Can you think of creative and whimsical ways to love others where you work, play, or study?

2. Why do you think people fear asking questions about faith, even in church?

3. Jesus was challenging old norms when he washed his disciples' feet. Are there norms that need to be challenged in your life?

4. "God is in the outcome business. We are in the obedience business." How might this apply in your life?

19

Do-overs

"Then Moses raised his arm and struck the rock twice with his staff.
Water gushed out, and the community and their livestock drank.
But the LORD said to Moses and Aaron, 'Because you did not trust
in me enough to honor me as holy in the sight of the Israelites,
you will not bring this community into the land I give them.'"

NUMBERS 20:11–12

"No do-overs" was a common refrain of our neighborhood games while growing up. It means no second chances, but no do-overs had to be said aloud by someone before the start of the contest. Otherwise, do-overs were totally in. In golf, they are called mulligans, and they aren't counted on your scorecard. My golf game is so weak that you could give me a mulligan on every hole, and I still wouldn't break 100. Wouldn't it be great if, in life, we could have a few do-overs to undo some of our worst mistakes and regrets? Unfortunately, it doesn't work that way.

If anyone deserved a life mulligan, it was Moses. God instructed him to speak to the rock, and water would gush out, but Moses struck the rock twice instead. I wasn't there, obviously, but I bet God said, "No do-overs" when he first spoke to Moses from the burning bush. God forgave Moses for this and many other wrong moves, but forgiveness differs from a mulligan. Moses's mistake had unpleasant consequences, and he was not allowed to enter the Promised Land. Our mistakes work the same way. God's grace covers all our sins but doesn't exempt us from their consequences. However, we've discovered something that comes pretty close to a mulligan ... being a grandparent.

Parenting versus Grandparenting

Every parent makes mistakes and wishes they would have done things differently. Our parenting improved as we got older, but we would do over many things if we could. Nobody gets through life without some regrets. I didn't realize until I got older that my mistakes could create unpleasant consequences for others. One of the more popular cultural lies is that what we do to or for ourselves does not harm others. The accepted illusion is that we are islands unto ourselves and have no impact or duty to others. One of those lies is that there are no consequences if we can't see them immediately. These illusions are shattered by any decent self-examination of our parenting or that of others.

My parents (aka Carl and Tootie) were not the same people who became grandparents. My brothers and I often wondered where these wonderful people were when we were growing up. If they make a Grandparents Hall of Fame, our mom and dad would be good candidates. They are first-ballot winners.

We learned a lot by watching them with our children. They seemed to find the perfect balance of love and discipline. I resolved to learn from our parents' example and the mistakes I made as a dad when it was my turn to be a grandparent. It felt like a do-over. I called it.

Chase

Our Kari married Steve Peterson in October 2001. It was one of the best days of all our lives, and it was a small, beautiful ceremony. My mom made the food; Jackie Roche, a good friend, brought and arranged the flowers; and Steve's grandmother hosted the ceremony at the clubhouse in her neighborhood. Steve Cathcart, our pastor, performed the ceremony. It was a beautiful fall day and a perfect way to begin their life together. A wedding doesn't have to be expensive to be memorable and beautiful. It was the people who made it special. Even now, it is my favorite wedding of all time.

A few years later, Kari was pregnant, and we were all anxiously awaiting our first grandchild. In April 2005, Chase Peterson was born ... twelve weeks early. He weighed less than three pounds, and my first impression as he was rushed down the hospital hallway was that he could be E.T.'s stunt double. He would spend the next five weeks in the Neonatal Intensive Care Unit (NICU).

During that time, we and countless others prayed for Chase to survive and thrive. Each day, he fought to live, conquering one health crisis after another. We knew the odds for survival weren't good, but we trusted God for the outcome. We believe he always has our best interest in mind, and we would accept it, no matter how things turned out for Chase and the family. "A snowball's chance in Hades" are odds we had become accustomed to. We are fighters; maybe that's where Chase got his tenacity from. When the time came for him to leave the NICU and come home, we were beginning to allow ourselves to think he would be okay. Many prayers of thanksgiving were offered.

Sharon and I were Nana and Pop Pop. Since that less-than-auspicious beginning, we have enjoyed and pressed into every opportunity to be excellent grandparents. Chase spent many weekends with us as a baby and toddler, and we took him on many trips by plane and car. We wanted Chase to know us and to feel loved unconditionally … to be loved as only grandparents can. We were channeling our "Carl and Tootie."

In 2014, we moved from Charlotte to Rock Hill, South Carolina, to be closer to the Petersons. Chase was growing up fast, and we knew if we were closer, we could be more helpful and more involved in the years he had left at home. This would be especially helpful because Kari and Steve's work schedules made school transportation difficult and often impossible. Nana and Pop Pop could be counted on to help. We were also there for special school events and other hobbies that Chase pursued.

When Chase became old enough to drive, he asked his Pop Pop to teach him. It had been many years since I taught Kari, but I agreed to help because I knew we'd get some good stories to share. I was not disappointed. One of our memorable lessons occurred while driving to school … well, in their driveway. Chase didn't feel like getting behind the wheel on this particular morning. His Nana would have let him slide, but not Pop Pop. "Too bad," I said. He got in, fastened his seatbelt, adjusted the mirrors, and put the car in drive. Unfortunately, he needed to back out of the driveway. Before Chase hit the gas, I asked him to turn off the ignition. "Get your head out of your butt." I said a different word, something that meant butt. He never told me he didn't feel like driving after that, but he did manage to pay me back by telling that story to the whole church one Sunday.

We've learned that not all grandparents like their or anybody's grandchildren. That's a tragedy, a profound loss for all parties. Our experience has been both a privilege and a blessing. We like other people's grandchildren, too. We've enjoyed Ben and Janelle Ganson's kids, Micah, Caleb, and Abby, and the latest additions, Marvens and Marvel from Haiti. We gave Micah his first lawn mowing gig, and I coached him with Ben in basketball. Caleb started baking the birthday cookies I sent to my advisory clients, and then we spread the word. He now has a very large following. I can't look at Marvens and Marvel without thanking God for our small part in their story.

Even though being grandparents or pseudo-grandparents isn't a perfect do-over, God does astounding work: He redeems what we've lost as a result of our mistakes, and he redeems some of those on this side of eternity.

Redemption

When we were kids, recycling existed, but we didn't call it that. We knew it as redeeming glass bottles for money. This was a common practice, as bottles were often reusable and could be returned to the store or distributor and redeemed for a few pennies. Many people threw those bottles away, and when riding bikes, we would find them along the side of the road. We bought a lot of baseball cards and bubble gum that way.

God is also in the redemption business, offering to exchange our mistakes and blunders for his immeasurable grace. Many believe God is in the condemnation business, but that's untrue. One of the definitions of "redeem" is to pay the money to clear a debt. That's exactly what Jesus's death on the cross did for us. He purchased our freedom, clearing our debt from sin, by laying down his sinless life in exchange for ours. Condemnation is the devil's work, and we often choose it by rejecting Jesus. "For God did not send his Son into the world to condemn the world, but to save the world through him"[80] is the verse that immediately follows the often-quoted John 3:16.

Common synonyms of redeem are deliver, ransom, reclaim, rescue, and save. God is an excellent reclaimer; he doesn't waste a thing, using even our past mistakes and exchanging them for something good now and in eternity. Even after Job lost his family and livelihood, the Lord eventually restored everything to him and doubled it. The prophet Joel spoke of God's promise to restore to Israel what the locusts had eaten;[81] we have experienced this in a fashion after the death of a close friend.

At Kari and Steve's wedding, the bride was in a bind with two dads. Which one walks her down the aisle? Fortunately, the solution was a little easier when they decided on a non-traditional ceremony outside. The bride and groom gathered at the front with our pastor, so no one needed to perform that function. Sharon and my wedding was similar. These life events are the stuff of hopes, dreams, and memory-making.

By his grace, however, God did something unexpected and quite generous. He arranged for me to be asked to walk my friend's daughter down the aisle. For many years, I was a Stephen Minister to Herb Burns. He was Kari's first hospital patient while in nursing school. Herb was battling cancer, and we met and talked often and became close. After his unfortunate death, his daughter Susan asked me to walk her down the aisle at her wedding. Susan is an only child, and I was thrilled to do this for her. It looked and felt like a gift to me from the Lord. On May 21, 2005, Matt Covington and Susan became husband and wife. The next day, our grandson Chase Peterson came home unexpectedly from the hospital NICU. It's hard to express all the emotions and the degree of gratitude I

80 John 3:17
81 Joel 2:25

felt that weekend. Looking through the eyes of faith and knowing Jesus the way I do, I recognized his loving gifts of unmerited favor for us. This is one small but powerful expression of what it looks like to "restore what the locusts have eaten" on this side of eternity. There is much more to come.

If you think your life is beyond redemption, have another think because you couldn't be more wrong. God is more merciful and gracious than we give him credit for, and don't let anyone tell you he can't save you or use you to partner with him in changing the world. Witness the life and failure of King David when he had an affair with his friend Uriah's wife, Bathsheba.[82]

When David learned Bathsheba was pregnant with his child, he arranged to have his friend killed in battle. Some friend! King David, the one the Bible says is "a man after God's own heart," is an adulterer and murderer.

God forgave a repented King David, but there were horrible consequences for him, his family, and the nation of Israel, including the death of the child. There was an undeniable spiritual law of sowing and reaping at work.

But God wasn't done with him. David married Bathsheba, and she gave birth to another child, Solomon. The lineage of Jesus, the world's Savior, has been traced back to David and Bathsheba through Solomon. This story should give everyone hope. God wants to redeem the world with you and me in it.

Groundhog Day

We recently rewatched the 1993 comedy/fantasy movie *Groundhog Day* with Bill Murray as cynical TV weatherman Phil Connors.[83]

---

82 2 Samuel 11–12
83 *Groundhog Day*, directed by Harold Ramis (Columbia Pictures, 1993).

Phil relives the same day repeatedly when he goes on location to the small town of Punxsutawney to film a report about their annual Groundhog Day. His predicament distracts him until he sees a way of exploiting the situation. He fails repeatedly, trapped in this endless cycle. Phil learns to forget about his selfish ego and accept the things he can't change, and he becomes a better person. This new approach to life pays off, as he wins the heart of Rita (Andie MacDowell) and finally escapes his imprisonment in Groundhog Day.

We all can resonate with Phil Connors as life often feels like an endless loop of daily difficulty. Life is hard, and it has built-in loops of sixty-second minutes, sixty-minute hours, twenty-four-hour days, and seven-day weeks. It is a mixed blessing of daily predictability combined with the challenges of daily living. We know the earth will complete its daily rotation and the sun will rise again in the morning. Life can often feel like Groundhog Day.

We, like Phil, awake to a day that looks a lot like yesterday. With each new day, we can start fresh, make the same or different choices … and shape a life with meaning, purpose, and joy. Perhaps God had something like that in mind when he set time in motion, and "his-story" began. He is a God who loves new beginnings, fresh starts, and to take what others want to discard and recreate something profoundly beautiful. It's not a do-over, like Groundhog Day, but it is the next best thing.

FINDING OUR PLACE
IN THE STORY

1. "Nobody gets through life without some regrets. God's grace covers all our sins but doesn't exempt us from their consequences." Can you explain the difference between forgiveness and unpleasant consequences?

2. "Common synonyms of redeem are deliver, ransom, reclaim, rescue, and save. God is an excellent reclaimer. He doesn't waste a thing." Can you think of any times in your life when God has redeemed a past mistake and made something beautiful from it?

3. Grandparenting isn't a perfect do-over, but it comes close. Can you think of any others?

4. Have you been told that God can't save you or use you to partner with him in changing the world? What encouragement can you take from the story of David and Bathsheba?

20

Doggy Do-over

"Then God said, 'I give you every seed-bearing plant on the face of the whole earth and every tree that has fruit with seed in it. They will be yours for food. And to all the beasts of the earth and all the birds in the sky and all the creatures that move along the ground—everything that has the breath of life in it—I give every green plant for food.' And it was so."

<small>Genesis 1:29–30</small>

We were blessed with many unique and interesting pets as a family. Our Kari's nickname was Ellie Mae, the animal-loving character from the Beverly Hillbillies. We had cats and dogs, but Kari also tried her hand at fish, birds, reptiles, rabbits, and ferrets. I can't think of any of our pets that would be considered normal. They were all characters, but one dog stood out— our Beauregard.

Soon after our grandson Chase was born, Kari talked me into rescuing a dog. She reasoned that it would be good for Chase, but I didn't need much encouragement when it came to adopting dogs or cats. A friend from work rescued boxers and helped me find Beauregard. Beau was eighty pounds of joy. He was handsome except for a few scars on his face and leg. He might have been three years old when we adopted him. When Chase was old enough to talk, he would tell people, "His first name is Beau, and his last name is Regard."

Beau was a push-button dog, meaning he was easy to train and would do anything I asked. Sometimes, all I had to do was look at him to communicate what I wanted, and he was eager to comply. He was always at my side or my feet. He followed me if I left a room, never letting me out of his sight or presence. When he looked at me, he always looked into my eyes, creating an amazing connection between us. He died in 2014, and I still miss him.

Because of the evidence, we're sure he was trained and used as a fight dog. There were the scars, of course, but also the time he played with the neighbor's two dogs when the play turned into fighting. The two dogs lost; Beau pinned them both to the ground, one on top of the other. Soon after, we noticed that he would have to lie down when he got overly excited. It looked like he was going to pass out. Our vet said he had a heart murmur. As he aged, it got worse, and his need to lie down after a little exercise increased in frequency and severity. His recovery time took longer after each episode. But when he did recover, he would get up as if nothing had happened, ready for the next adventure.

Beau was crate-trained and spent most of the weekdays there while we were at work. That guilt you feel when you abandon your pet, even for a few hours, never abated. Vacations were especially difficult because Beau didn't get along well with other dogs, and we hated to board him. There were a few times when we vacationed at the beach and were able to take him with us. Beau loved it there, and so did we. To say this was a cherished family pet would be an understatement.

We liked to invite others to join us on our beach trips because the place we stayed at had five bedrooms. One year, our friend

Mark joined us. Mark was single and in his twenties and made the trip down from his home in Pennsylvania. We played many board games together, and he even taught Chase how to master the Rubik's Cube.

Our first morning there, we gathered up all our gear and made our way to the ocean. The surf was pounding the shore, and the sound of the waves drowned out our voices. I had the strap attached to a beach chair draped over each shoulder and a cup of coffee in each hand as we made our way over the dunes and down to the beach. Mark and Beau had taken off ahead of the rest of us. I could see them running around and playing with gusto. I tried to warn Mark about Beau's heart condition, but he couldn't hear me over the sound of the surf. By the time I caught up with them, it was too late. Beau began to stagger and wobble, and as he approached me, he did a face-plant into the sand. Our family pet had stopped breathing, and he was gone. Beau was dead.

I kneeled next to my dead dog as Mark and the rest of the family stood there in disbelief. It's funny what can run through your mind at such times. *Oh no, Mark's going to feel awful about killing our dog,* I thought. Then, *I wonder if I can bury Beau in a dune. When we get home, I can finally paint our bedroom and cover up all of Beau's slobber. Maybe we can replace the carpet.*

With everyone's eyes on me, I felt like I had to do something. *Mouth to mouth?* I wondered as I stared down at his slobber and sand-filled lips. No, not an option. All I could think to do was to begin to do some chest compressions. I began to pound on his boxer barrel chest with increasing intensity. This was turning out to be the start of a horrible vacation.

Like a bolt of electricity, Beau's legs started to shake vigorously. I couldn't believe my eyes; our Beau was trying to return to life. For the next two hours, Beau lay there, unable to move. But when his heart allowed it, he got up and acted like nothing had happened. Now that's a do-over!

We didn't want to talk about it and make Mark feel bad. We never mentioned it even after that vacation. We always wondered if Mark knew that Beau had died on that beach. That mystery was cleared up for us on his wedding day. When Mark married his bride, Gretta, we made the trip to Washington, DC, to witness the blessed occasion. Sharon and I didn't know anyone other than the bride and groom. Mark's sister took pity on us and introduced us to their parents. His parents looked puzzled when they met us. Obviously, the Jette name didn't register. That is, until Mark's sister said, "These are the Jettes. Remember, Mark killed their dog." We could see instant recognition on their faces. *Oh, those Jettes.* Mystery solved. We weren't the only ones telling that story to others.

After that beach trip, Beau lived another four years before we said our final goodbyes. Will we see our beloved pets again in the new heaven and new earth? Man, I hope so. It's hard to imagine that the God of all creation, who made such special and cherished animals, would not include them in his new and final creation. Whenever one of our pets died or had to be put down, we cried and mourned for our loss. Many years have passed, and we still miss them. We know there will be no more death, mourning, crying, or pain in the new creation, so how could they not be included in God's final do-over? (Maybe not ferrets; they had to be a mistake.)

FINDING OUR PLACE
IN THE STORY

1. Pets and other animals have a special place in many lives. They can also be expensive to maintain and manage. Why do you think God included them in his initial creation?

2. Have you ever had to decide to end the life of your cherished pet? How did it feel to have the power of life and death over another creature?

3. How do you imagine our Creator feels about his creatures?

4. The Bible doesn't say if we will see our beloved animals again in the new heaven and new earth. Can you think of any clues in the Bible that would lead you to think that we will have them with us?

21

Church Reimagined

*"Jesus answered them, 'It is not the healthy
who need a doctor, but the sick.'"*

LUKE 5:31

Every religion believes God loves good people, but the radical
message of the gospel is that God loves bad people. That is
good news for people like me. Jesus avoided the religious types
and spent most of his time with prostitutes, tax collectors, adul-
terers, and a few fishermen. From the beginning, Jesus called all
broken people to repentance and forgiveness. Church is a hospital
for sinners, not a museum for saints, and I freely admit my need
for healing and redemption. Jesus exchanges our junk for his grace
and invites us to partner with him through a community we call
the Church.

The word translated as "church" in the English Bible from the
original Greek manuscripts is ekklesia. This is the Greek word
"kaleo" (to call), with the prefix "ek" (out), or the called-out ones.[84]
Someone who attends a church doesn't always equate to being a
follower of Jesus. The called-out ones are invited into a family. I
attended church for years before I was born again and adopted into

---

84 "1577. ekklésia," BibleHub.com, accessed July 25, 2024, https://biblehub.com
/greek/1577.htm.

the family of God. There is a profound difference between being religious and having a relationship with Jesus.

My parents and grandparents were Catholic, so I went to church even before I was born. Our family was St. Mary's Catholic Church members in Swormville, New York. I was the youngest of four boys, and we attended St. Mary's Grade School from first through eighth grade. Every school day began with Mass. We were altar boys and members of the children's choir. My two oldest brothers, Carl and Alan, left home in ninth grade to attend Catholic Seminaries (neither became a priest). My brother David and I attended Bishop Neumann Catholic High School. Add it up: that's a lot of religion classes and church! And more than our share of fish because Catholics didn't eat meat on Fridays. That's probably why my Southern Baptist father-in-law wasn't thrilled to hear his daughter was marrying a "mackerel snapper." (But he did love me anyway.)

What do you get when you combine a Catholic with a Southern Baptist? A Presbyterian. At least, that's what someone suggested when we started as a new family and married couple. Neither of us was comfortable inside the other's church denomination, so we took the advice and started visiting a Presbyterian church when we lived in Raleigh, North Carolina. It worked for us; we identified as Presbyterians for thirty years. In that time, I have been an ordained deacon and elder and served on numerous committees. Whenever the church doors were open, the Jettes were there. We've been part of the Vineyard movement for the last ten years since moving to Rock Hill and meeting Ben Ganson.

If I had to find a label to fit my churchgoing style, it could be "presbycostal," someone equally comfortable in formal and much less formal settings. I love the liturgy of Catholic Mass, the Presbyterian's devotion to the scriptures, and the freedom of worship of the Pentecostals. I'm not a church expert, but I have a unique perspective.

Whenever I attend a Catholic Mass now, I am moved by the liturgy and the celebration of the Lord's Supper, things I took for granted while growing up. Our thirty years with Presbyterianism have shaped our spiritual growth because of their emphasis on the study of the Bible. Reading, studying, and memorizing God's Word helped me fall in love with Jesus. One of the not-so-flattering descriptions of the Presbyterian church is "the frozen chosen." That's not something the Vineyard movement could be convicted of. We appreciate how the Vineyard marries the inspiration of scripture with the freedom and power of the Holy Spirit. Most Rock Hill Vineyard weekly church services occur in people's homes.

House church is light years from my Roman Catholic roots. It is a far cry from the Presbyterian mantra, "Decently and in order." In a word, the house church experience is "messy." It's challenging to have all ages in the same room simultaneously. It can be loud and distracting at times. In house church, it is hard to hide; not only does everyone get to "play," but everyone has to play. People must host, help with worship, or lead discussions in their homes. There is no sermon. I describe our version of the sermon as a spiritual covered-dish supper. Instead of meat, potatoes, and dessert, we study the same Bible passage all week and bring something from our study to share on Sunday.

One of the common criticisms of the major denominations and some mega-churches is that they tend to produce shallow followers—a mile wide but an inch deep. It shouldn't be too surprising that, in our house church experience, people are becoming noticeably more spiritually mature, including our children. We don't have members, so you can't join, but you can belong. Belonging is what happens in families. We are small but mighty.

The Church's Mission—New Creation

Jesus's mission centered on the coming of God's Kingdom and restoring God's rule over all creation and human life. In their book *The True Story of the Whole World*, Michael Goheen and Craig Bartholomew capture the essence of Christ's mission: "In his life, Jesus embodied the kingdom. In his words, he announced the kingdom, and in his actions, he demonstrated that the kingdom had come. He welcomed the marginalized, formed a kingdom community, taught by precept and example how to live faithfully within that community, and suffered for its sake as he challenged the idolatrous culture of his time. And he prayed for the kingdom. All of this shapes our mission today as we follow Jesus."[85] The Church reimagined is a paradigm shift where we see that everything we do with and for Jesus is part of the new creation. *It all counts for eternity . . . not just Sundays.*

Jesus's preaching centered on the Kingdom of God, which is mentioned 126 times in the Gospels.[86] His Kingdom would grow and spread incrementally, often imperceptibly. This King would conquer with love, and his loyal subjects would be known for their love. After his ascension, the Church would be his instrument and representative to continue the mission.

---

85 Craig Bartholomew and Michael W. Goheen, *The True Story of the Whole World: Finding Your Place in the Biblical Drama* (Grand Rapids, MI: Faith Alive Christian Resources, 2009).

86 John Piper, "What Is the Kingdom of God?" desiringGod.org, September 8, 2017, https://www.desiringgod.org/interviews/what-is-the-kingdom-of-god.

The Church Reimagined

The declining membership of the church in America and Europe has been well-documented by researchers and pundits. They want you and me to believe the Christian church is dying. Their reports are reminiscent of the story of the blind men and the elephant. The blind men have never heard of an elephant before, and each one imagines what it is like by touching it. Each blind man feels a different part of the elephant's body, but only one part, such as the side, the tusk, or the tail. They then describe the elephant based on their limited experience, and their descriptions of the elephant differ. The story's moral is that humans claim to know something to its fullest based on their limited, subjective experience.

What the researchers and media pundits overlook is that the head of the church, Jesus, is still alive. The church isn't dying and will never die because Jesus isn't dead. The church continues to grow and thrive all around the world. Only one person can see the whole elephant: Jesus. And he isn't worried. He is still King of kings and is seated on the throne at the Father's right hand. No one other than Jesus can hope to accurately assess the church's past, present, or future impact on building his Kingdom and fulfilling his mission.

Can We Talk?

As Mom often said, "Getting older is not for sissies." You could easily say the same thing about belonging to a church. We learned to love the Lord's Church with all its imperfections and brokenness. Being a contributing part of a church is challenging and complicated. Joan Rivers developed numerous classic bits and catchphrases through her decades of entertaining on stage and screen, but three small words stand above the rest: "Can we talk?"[87] It was an invitation to her audience, signaling she was about to confide in them.

We know firsthand the many flaws and failures of a church. As a family and couple, we have often been the bullseye for church members' target practice. Those arrows hurt. We heard it said that the Christian church is the only army in the world that shoots its own wounded. It's all true because, remember, the church is full of bad people like me. It is more of a hospital for sinners than a museum for saints. Being a contributing member of a biblical and broken community of Jesus's followers is hard but also good. It is reminiscent of what people say about marriage being "hard work." Church leadership/membership and marriage are not as much hard work as they are "good work."

The Church reimagined is perceiving how God is co-laboring powerfully with and through his people to accomplish the mission. Here are a few examples to help illustrate how God is working:

- I know a brother in Christ who started a business in a country most would consider unsafe. He works in that location because God put love in his heart for the people there. He is showing the love of the Father by creating the opportunity for humans to flourish through the business. In a culture that values corruption and bribes, their business is a light of transparency, integrity, and honesty.

- I know a brother in Christ who started a new business at age twenty-five and hired two men to help him. He shows God's love by focusing on their welfare, keeping them working, paying them well, giving bonuses, ministering to their families, and helping them with immigration issues so they can become citizens. He gave them English-Spanish Bibles for Christmas.

- I know a husband and wife who follow Jesus and already had three children when they began adopting others from around the world. Today, they are the parents of twelve. They seek and adopt children with special needs, including children with no arms or legs. They choose them *because* of their disabilities, which mirrors what God does when he adopts us. We need rescuing, too.

- I know a church family that helps take care of the needs of a member with cerebral palsy. He has outlived his parents, but the members of this church make sure he knows how much he is loved. They take him to doctor's appointments, shopping, church, breakfast, and even to see his favorite sports team beat the Carolina Panthers.

- I know a group of Jesus followers who met in the basement of a coffee shop every Monday for many years, praying for their city and those living in the margins. Out of the saltiness of those prayers, God is transforming how the city serves the homeless and working poor. Nonprofit ministries, churches, local government agencies, and businesses work together with a gospel focus. And it all began because God's people prayed.

- I have been involved in gospel mission organizations that focus on relief services when natural and unnatural disasters strike. We repair structures, build wells for clean water, and connect people to desperately needed sources of capital. We show up in places where Christians aren't allowed or safe.

- I know brothers and sisters in Christ who teach in government schools and share the love of Jesus with their students and colleagues. I know of ministries that teach the Bible in public schools and give food to students to take home on the weekends because there is not enough to eat at home.

- I know brothers and sisters in Christ who have started private Christian schools because the government schools are failing our kids. Their schools are growing so fast that they need more classrooms.

- I know of multiple food pantries and feeding programs in town financed and operated by followers of Jesus who believed him when he said, "Whatever you did for one of the least of these brothers and sisters of mine, you did for me."[88]

- I know street children in Honduras who have found hope and a place to live, thanks to a group of Jesus's followers who decided to help twenty-four years ago. Today, they also provide accelerated, year-long classroom instruction and hands-on training programs to help street-connected youth acquire the skills necessary to step away from the streets and enter the workforce.

- I know a husband and wife who, in 1991, left comfort and security with three small children to fulfill a vision for which they had prayed for over twenty years. In the Great

---

[88] Matthew 25:40

Smoky Mountains in Tennessee, they established a ranch to provide homes, education, and counseling for children from difficult family situations. The ministry has grown and prospered and is now led by one of their children.

- I know a Christian brother who, on November 10, 1990, was diagnosed with brain cancer and told to get his affairs in order. Twenty-seven years later, with surgery, two years of chemotherapy, and thirty rounds of radiation, he turned his experience into ministry. He has developed a leading-edge methodology for aftercare for those with terminal cancer, where many patients outlive their prognoses by years as he has.

- I know fellow Jesus followers working in the hospitals, police stations, fire stations, schools (public, private, and home schools), and businesses in my city. Everywhere we go, we take Jesus and his love with us.

Be encouraged! Our presence, his Spirit, and his love become like a new strand of DNA, changing the nature of everything around us. This is just a partial list, the tip of the iceberg. Multiply these stories by millions over millennia, and we would still only have a glimpse of what God is doing! Can you re-imagine it?

We have been privileged to visit and worship with other brothers and sisters in Christ in Jamaica, Haiti, Zambia, and Malawi. The global church is a family; without exception, wherever we have gone, we have experienced family unity: "There is one body and one Spirit, just as you were called to one hope when you were called; one Lord, one faith, one baptism; one God and Father of all, who is over all and through all and in all."[89]

---

89 Ephesians 4:4–6

There are millions of reasons to be hopeful and ready when the trumpet sounds at the end of history and Christ returns. God has promised the reunification of heaven and earth, and God himself dwelling with all humankind from every nation; no more sin, sickness, pain, or death. Love and justice reign, and a renewed creation will be healed, liberated, and restored. New creation. I can't wait! Come, Lord Jesus!

FINDING OUR PLACE
IN THE STORY

1. "Every religion believes God loves good people, but the radical message of the gospel is that God loves bad people." How can God possibly love bad people?

2. "Someone who attends church doesn't always equate to being a follower of Jesus." How do we know if it is Jesus we are following and not a set of rules or religious traditions?

3. The house church model is messy. What parts of it, if any, interested you?

4. "The Church reimagined is a paradigm shift where we see that everything we do with and for Jesus is part of the new creation." How do you find the sacred in the secular?

5. We have many reasons to be hopeful about the Church's future and mission—a new creation. Make a list of the evidence you have witnessed that gives you hope.

22

Blessing the City

*"Also, seek the peace and prosperity of the city to which
I have carried you into exile. Pray to the Lord for it,
because if it prospers, you too will prosper."*

JEREMIAH 29:7

We moved to Rock Hill, South Carolina, from Charlotte, North Carolina, in the summer of 2014. The overarching reason for moving was to be geographically closer to our daughter, Kari, her husband, Steve, and our grandson, Chase. We were being called on to help in various ways, and it made more sense for us to live in Rock Hill. Moving was familiar territory for Sharon and me, but we had lived in Charlotte for twenty-five years by now.

We weren't only changing our residence; we were changing states and cities. Sharon worked primarily from home, but our new house was eighteen miles from my office, which was still in Charlotte. It was a short move when measured in miles, but Rock Hill is vastly different from Charlotte. While we appreciated the lower property taxes and cheaper gas in Rock Hill, we had invested twenty-five years of our lives in Charlotte. The short distance betrayed the significance of the move.

Commuting in larger cities is challenging. Traffic in Charlotte has grown increasingly congested since we moved there in 1989.

I knew the commute to Charlotte would be a headache. The trip from our new home in Rock Hill to my office in Charlotte, in good rush hour traffic, took forty-five minutes. You could add another thirty minutes on some days because of traffic congestion and accidents. This new reality was intolerable for me. After a few weeks of trying different routes and departure times, I settled on a schedule consisting of getting up at 4:30 a.m. and arriving at the office between 5:30 and 6:00. It wasn't ideal, but I could get to work in about twenty minutes. I could also leave earlier to miss the worst rush hour traffic in the afternoon. When I asked Ben Ganson to join me in practice part-time in 2015, his hours were 9:30 to 2:30, which worked well for him, as he was also commuting from Rock Hill.

We both felt called to invest more in Rock Hill, and commuting daily to Charlotte made that more difficult. One of those investments involved Ben's other job. He led a group that planted the Vineyard Church in Rock Hill, which Sharon and I attended.

Another was the prayer group Ben and I initiated to pray for our city every Monday morning in the basement of Amelie's bakery and coffee shop. Every great move of God begins with prayer. For much of my life, I thought prayers were a way of getting God on my agenda; now, I know he uses prayer to help us align with his plan. This is illustrated most powerfully in how he orchestrated the creation of the Pathways Community Center in Rock Hill to help those living in or near poverty.

Ben and I heard about a few men working with people experiencing homelessness in our community who were discouraged. We took the men to coffee and prayed for them. As we got to know them better, we met more frequently to pray and encourage them. We knew that if God placed the plight of the homeless on our hearts, he also would have told others and helped lead us to them. Over time, others were invited, and we prayed every Monday morning in that basement. We asked the Father for the same thing that Jesus did in the Lord's Prayer, "Transform our city on earth as it is in heaven." We prayed into seven areas of focus: poverty, family, church unity, education, justice, racial reconciliation, and the marketplace. We were battling the enemy of our souls for the heart of our community.

Poverty

Jesus revealed the heart of the Father toward the "least of these" when he spoke of the separating of the sheep and the goats at the end of time, saying: "Then the righteous will answer him, 'Lord, when did we see you hungry and feed you, or thirsty and give you something to drink? When did we see you a stranger and invite you in, or needing clothes and clothe you? When did we see you sick or in prison and go to visit you?' The King will reply, 'Truly I tell you, whatever you did for one of the least of these brothers and sisters of mine, you did for me.'"[90] If you want to see God turn water into wine, ask what hurts his heart, and keep praying.

After a few years of praying together, miraculous things began to happen. Like seeds planted in fertile soil or after the gestation period of pregnancy ... from an underground basement ... God brought forth Pathways Community Center. (We know God had other groups and individuals praying for the poor in our city, too.) Pathways started in 2017 when God brought together a visionary group of business, church, government, nonprofit, and community leaders to create a solution for people in poverty. Two prayer team members were invited to be on the inaugural board and were an integral part of the start-up. One of those was Ben.

90 Matthew 25:37–45

By 2019, the Pathways Board had designed a systematic solution to align resources, data, and service agencies to address the gaps in essential services. They brought together a network of existing service agencies to operate on-site while collaborating with other health and human service providers, creating one-stop access for people. "They recognized the potential of the ninety-eight-year-old West End Elementary School, a forty thousand square foot building, to serve as a beacon of hope for the community. Together, they breathed life into the building, pouring their hearts and souls into its revival. The building's transformation reflected the transformative journey of the town itself. Through compassion, education, and unity, the wounds of the past were healed, and a brighter future was envisioned."[91] Today, Pathways is housing a homeless day shelter, men's shelter, women's shelter, food pantry, meal programs, and more.

Each year, God has continued to improve and expand Pathway's collaboration and impact. The momentum is astounding; the "least" are being loved and served because God's people heard what was on his heart and were moved to their knees. He can do more in five seconds than we can do in five hours, months, or years.

The Marketplace

As we prayed about God's work in the marketplace, Ben and I frequently asked if he wanted us to have an office in Rock Hill. Opening an office would be expensive and risky, but increasing our presence in Rock Hill would be another way for us to bless our new city. One of our Monday prayer partners was a commercial contractor willing to lease us a couple of cubicles in his

---

91 "Our Commitment," Pathways, pathwaysyc.org, accessed July 25, 2024, https://www.pathwaysyc.org/about.

newly renovated office. The rent was reasonable and would give us much-needed flexibility each week. I always sought wise counsel before making significant business decisions, so I ran the idea by Larry Carroll. Larry was born and raised in Rock Hill but lived in Charlotte. He liked the idea and thought it was a low-risk way to test the waters. In August of 2017, we began working in Rock Hill two days a week.

The contractor's newly renovated space was lovely, and his employees were friendly, but boy, was it ever loud. The combination of an open ceiling and concrete floor caused sound to reverberate; at times, the noise was deafening. In February 2018, we made a similar arrangement with a small local CPA firm and set up shop there instead. It wasn't ideal, either, but it was a start, and we continued to pray for God's will.

In 2019, Larry's son, Kris, approached me with a proposition. He and Larry were considering opening a small office in Rock Hill and wanted to know if I would be interested in selling my practice to them and moving Ben's and my office there. They had many clients who lived in that area, and he spent time teaching in the business school at the local university. Kris thought it could be a win-win. Ben and I certainly didn't see that coming, but it was clear that God was up to something, so we prayerfully agreed on the terms and joined forces.

Kris began looking for office space and would run various scenarios by us periodically. He was going to hire a person to work in the new office in an administrative role to support him and us. We were encouraged by every option he shared because we were anxious to begin working in the new Carroll Financial Rock Hill office.

But God, once again, was about to surprise us. One day, Kris dropped by my office and closed the door to tell me they had purchased a substantial accounting and investment practice in

FOLLOWING THE INVISIBLE JESUS

Rock Hill. Our office needs had just become a whole lot bigger. In February 2020, we moved into one of the most prestigious office buildings in the city, fully equipped with new modern furniture and five new colleagues.

The Bible says that God's ways are not our ways. In March, one month after our new office open house, COVID-19 hit. Come on! That was disappointing on many levels. At first, we worked from home, but everyone returned after a few weeks. COVID changed a lot of well-worn behaviors, not the least of which was having client meetings in person. Before COVID, it was rare to have virtual meetings with clients, and Zoom was something you did to pass another car on the interstate.

The COVID hangovers weren't all bad; some things changed for the better. Because of COVID-19, even the least technologically savvy learned to engage in Zoom meetings.

When life began to return to normal, we offered clients and prospects the option of meeting in our first-class office spaces in Charlotte or Rock Hill or online. Our trips to Charlotte were greatly reduced, saving time, energy, and commuting headaches.

The most significant change had little to do with commuting and everything to do with our identity. We were becoming "Rock Hilligans," ... living, worshipping, and working in Rock Hill with increasing opportunities to bless and influence our community. I think this is what Jesus meant when he said, "The kingdom of heaven is like yeast that a woman took and mixed into about sixty pounds of flour until it worked all through the dough."[92] Little by little, we seek to bless more and more of our community.

Obviously, this is only a glimpse into what God can do through his people to bless our cities. We are continually amazed that he

---

92 Matthew 13:33

chooses people like us, broken and imperfect, to be his ambassadors. All the evidence confirmed that he wanted us to invest more of ourselves in Rock Hill, moving our business there in his way and his timing. With each passing day, he weaves us all into the fabric of our community as we work for its prosperity, seeking to make a difference. Experiences like this can be a happy reminder of God's sovereign grace, timing, and goodness. Followers of Jesus can certainly identify with Jim Harbaugh, the football coach, when he said, "Who's got it better than us?"[93]

---

93 Kevin Skiver, "Explaining Jim Harbaugh's 'Who's got it better than us?' rally cry as Michigan enters CFP," *Detroit Free Press*, January 8, 2024, https://www.freep .com/story/sports/college/university-michigan/2024/01/08/jim-harbaugh -whos-got-it-better-than-us-michigan-vs-washington-cfp-2024/72133093007/.

FINDING OUR PLACE
IN THE STORY

1. Every great move of God begins with prayer. How can you join others in your city to pray for its transformation?

2. What would your home, neighborhood, town, or city look like if his will was done "as it is in heaven"? How will you pray into that to help make it a reality?

3. The Bible says that God's ways are not our ways. What changed for the better after COVID-19 where you live?

4. How is God weaving you and others into the fabric of your community to work for its prosperity?

23

Blessing Others

"The Lord had said to Abram, 'Go from your country, your
people and your father's household to the land I will show you.
I will make you into a great nation, and I will bless you;
I will make your name great, and you will be a blessing.'"

GENESIS 12:1–2

When we moved to Rock Hill, we were the first family in the
Riverwalk neighborhood to move into the new Herrons
Ferry Road section. Riverwalk was a new development on the
banks of the Catawba River, and we were looking forward to this
next season of life. The development included miles of walking
and bike trails, a velodrome, a BMX track, a criterium course, a
YMCA, an amphitheater, and dozens of bike-friendly streets. The
homes are Craftsman style with Charleston-type colors and feel.
We bought a one-story ranch and settled in among all the mud,
ongoing construction, and partially paved streets and alleys.

Because we were the first to occupy a home, we dreamed of
ways to welcome our new neighbors when it was their turn to
move in. One of my favorite movie scenes in *It's a Wonderful Life*
is the welcome and dedication of the Martini family's new home.[94]

---

94 *It's a Wonderful Life*, directed by Frank Capra (RKO Pictures, Paramount Pictures, Republic Pictures, 1947).

George and Mary Bailey are standing at the entrance of the home, and they present the Martinis with three gifts and blessings:

> "BREAD that this house may never know hunger.
> SALT that life may always have flavor, and WINE
> that joy and prosperity may reign forever."

The appeal of this message for us was that it communicated more than just a welcome. It also said, "We want God to bless you." I went to the local Publix and bought a loaf of French bread, a twenty-six-ounce container of salt, a bottle of wine, and a gift bag to put them all in. I made a welcome card with a picture of the movie scene on the cover and the blessing message inside. We tied the card to the bag with a ribbon and included our names and phone numbers. Sharing this information allowed us to let them know they could count on us for help if they needed it.

Sharon thought it was all a little bit crazy, but she went along with me to our first new neighbors. When we got to their house, they were still moving things in. Their names were Alan and Candace, and they greeted us warmly. I helped Alan carry in a big-screen TV. Years later, when Candace and Alan were moving out, Candace told me how much our gift and gesture meant to them. She showed me the welcome card and blessing. She kept it as a reminder of how much they loved living there.

This scene was repeated a couple dozen times as the construction of each new home was completed and the new owners moved in. (The blessing bags, not the carrying of the big-screen TV.) We discovered this was also an effective way to learn our neighbors' names.

At the time of our first Thanksgiving in Riverwalk, many homes were in different construction phases. Three builders worked on our street, and most of the contractors' crews were hard-working

Hispanic men. We heard a crew hard at work across the street from us during Thanksgiving dinner. As the light of day faded and the dark of night crept in, the men were working by the headlights of their trucks and vans. Their families would not be celebrating with them this Thanksgiving. It broke our hearts.

Not wanting to see a repeat of this scene at Christmas, we were inspired to find a way to bless these hard workers. I mentioned our idea to Lawrence Lewis, a new neighbor, and a caper began to take shape. The idea was to treat these men to a meal close to Christmas Day. We approached all three builders and asked if they would let us serve them this way. We didn't want anything from them; we just wanted to bless them and say, "Thank you for all your hard work." The meal would include hot dogs, hamburgers, chips, tea, and homemade desserts. All the new residents on Herrons Ferry wanted to help and brought the desserts, and many helped with cooking, serving, and cleaning up. We picked a day, and the builders got the word out. We had no clue how many people would show up.

God blessed us with a beautiful mid-December afternoon on the event day. Lawrence fired up his three grills, and we put out borrowed tables and chairs with red tablecloths. When the appointed time to eat arrived, we watched as men began to come from all directions. It reminded me of a scene from the movie *Field of Dreams*, when the ball players would emerge from a cornfield, dressed in their baseball uniforms, and take their place on the diamond before the fun began.[95] The coming, dining, and going went on for a few hours. When it was over, we had served three hundred hamburgers and three hundred hot dogs. One of the foremen told

---

95 *Field of Dreams*, directed by Phil Alden Robinson (Universal Pictures, Carolco Pictures, 1989).

us that no one had ever done anything like this for them. He was clearly moved.

The Bible says the children of Abraham are people from all nations who put their hope in Jesus Christ. When we use God's blessings to love our neighbors, we are helping to fulfill God's promise to Abraham to bless all nations through him. In the Bible, when someone else's love and generosity touch people, they express their gratitude to God. I love that God gets all the credit and the glory. That Christmas, well over a hundred souls thanked God for a small lunch and a large helping of thoughtfulness from people they didn't know and would probably never see again—a Christmas present blessing wrapped up in a small lunch package.

FINDING OUR PLACE
IN THE STORY

1. We are blessed to be a blessing. When you read this chapter, did you imagine how you might use one of your gifts to bless others?

2. "We dreamed of ways to welcome our new neighbors." How is God inspiring you to greater levels of hospitality?

3. How do you feel about the risk of looking foolish when you do things out of your comfort zone to bless others?

4. "As the light of day faded and the dark of night crept in, the men were working by the headlights of their trucks and vans. Their families would not be celebrating with them this Thanksgiving. It broke our hearts." How can you engage with others in situations that break your heart?

24

How Much Is Enough?

*"I have learned to be content whatever the circumstances. I know
what it is to be in need, and I know what it is to have plenty. I have
learned the secret of being content in any and every situation ..."*

PHILIPPIANS 4:11–12

Enough. Contentment. It's not something we typically aspire to in our culture. I'm more acquainted with the "more is better" movement. Ron Blue was the first person I heard ask, "How much is enough?"[96] He was counseling his clients and friends to set specific wealth accumulation finish lines. Before I could answer Ron's question, I had to wrestle with a similar one: How much do I need before it is "safe" for me to stop accumulating?

Those of us in the United States live in the wealthiest nation in the history of the world. Even those of us who don't consider ourselves wealthy by American standards enjoy a higher standard of living than almost everyone else on the planet. Even so, I know it is impossible to accumulate enough wealth to be safe because there will always be risks beyond our means. Even Steve Jobs, one of the founders of Apple, wasn't able to utilize his gifts and resources to beat cancer. The world isn't safe. We can never accumulate enough

---

96 Ron Blue, "How Much is Enough?" Ron Blue Institute, January 31, 2017, https://ronblueinstitute.com/article/how-much-is-enough/.

to be safe and cover every conceivable risk, not to mention the ones we can't conceive. If that's true, why would we stop accumulating or doing what Jesus called "building bigger barns"?[97] Why did he call it foolish? Jesus was pointing out the folly of wealth accumulation as a means of eliminating our need for God, of feeling like masters of the universe, and of succumbing to the illusion of our control and ownership.

The Bible teaches that God is the owner of all things and the source of all provision. We are stewards or temporary managers. As managers, we know that money and things we accumulate or give away are not and never were ours. They are his. Our motivation for spending, saving, or giving begins with understanding our role as those with temporary custody. The day we die, we will only be able to take the things we own with us, the things we brought with us when we were born: Nothing. Nada. Zilch. Our opportunity in this temporal world is to prove ourselves excellent in stewarding all he has entrusted us with as preparation for the world to come. We can be generous, and we can experience real contentment because our Father in heaven is good, and he is worthy of our trust and dependence.

The biggest threats to our contentment are the twin two-sided coins of greed/envy and fear/scarcity. As people of faith, we can conquer these twin thieves by cultivating a stewardship and abundance mindset. The antidote to greed and envy is stripping wealth and money of its grip on us by growing in generosity. Nothing says "I'm a master over money" better than giving it away. By developing an abundance mentality, we experience God as extravagant in generosity, beginning with his inexhaustible grace. He is the One who loved the world and gave his only Son to rescue us from

97 Luke 12:16–21

sin and death. He wants us to trust him and not ourselves or our 401(k). Jesus said he came to give us an abundant life—life to the full.[98] The antidote to fear and scarcity thinking is faith.

The Apostle Paul wrote that he learned to be content, meaning it did not come naturally to him. It doesn't to you and me either. Greed and scarcity mindsets are win-lose paradigms; the enemy loves it when we focus on winning or losing. Faith teaches that God is our provider and that what others have or don't have is independent of our provision. In God's abundance, the pie always gets bigger, in contrast to the scarcity mindset, where there are only a limited number of slices to go around. Faith gives us the courage and freedom to share with others because we trust the One who provides for us. Then God does something surprising; he unleashes joy.

So, how much is enough? Over twenty years ago, Sharon and I began setting annual finish lines. This was good practice for when it came time to set a lifetime accumulation goal. Recently, by God's grace, we miraculously achieved this. It was a miracle. Each time we set a finish line, it seemed unobtainable. God would have to provide because of what we were giving away annually. Providing for us was no hardship to a God who owns it all. He was never worried. The question with each finish line we set is: "Do we trust him to provide for us if we don't have enough?" Every finish line gives me sweaty palms. Faith is still spelled R I S K. But Jesus is still turning water into wine.

We don't mind telling you that it is not easy to stop after a lifetime habit of accumulating. The secret sauce in setting finish lines is disarming the threats of greed, envy, fear, and scarcity by resolving these critical questions in advance. When we make peace with the

---

98 John 10:10

answers in our hearts before they become a reality, we rob them of their power to steal our contentment and peace.

Since we answered the question of how much is enough, we can be more like God in our generosity. One hundred percent of my author proceeds from this book are donated to some of our favorite charities. It is fun for us to think about all that God is going to do with these gifts and the people he will bless. We are grateful for your partnership by purchasing our book. On the other side of eternity, all he did with these gifts will be revealed, and we will celebrate together. Let's plan on meeting at Starrybucks for a cup of coffee.

FINDING OUR PLACE
IN THE STORY

1. The world isn't safe. We can never accumulate enough to be safe and cover every conceivable risk, not to mention the ones we can't conceive. If that's true:

    - Why would we stop accumulating or what Jesus called "building bigger barns?"[99]

    - Why did he call it foolish?

2. What is the antidote to greed and envy? What is the secret sauce?

3. The question with each finish line set is: "Do we trust him to provide for us if we don't have enough?"

4. How much is enough in your context?

---

99 Luke 12:16–21

25

Praying On Purpose

"Your Father knows what you need before you ask him. This, then, is how you should pray: "Our Father in heaven, hallowed be your name ..."

MATTHEW 6:8–9

Let's be real: prayer is mysterious and unnatural. When we pray, we communicate with someone we can't see but believe by faith that he exists and hears us. Jesus said his followers could hear him and know his voice.[100] Communication, even in prayer, is both speaking and listening. These realities make it hard to pray, so I've found it helpful to keep making changes in my prayer practice and will continue to tinker with it until the day I die. It makes sense if you consider prayer in the context of all forms of communication. We don't still talk like we did when we were toddlers or even teenagers, do we? Our ability to communicate with one another grows and evolves with our maturity, experience, and education. The closeness and nature of the relationship shape our communication, too. The Apostle Paul said we should pray without ceasing.[101] In my mind, to pray without ceasing is to live Coram Deo ... before the face of God. It is a way of living. As

---

100 John 10:27
101 1 Thessalonians 5:17 (NKJV)

I was writing this book, I often heard from God in the wee hours of the morning. It was a time, it seems, that I was available, and he would feed my writing thoughts and edits. Was that prayer? Absolutely, we were communicating with one another. Coram Deo is a life rhythm, like breathing.

In this chapter, I'm sharing a way of praying I use every morning and some of the whys or whats that went into my thinking. Socrates said, "The unexamined life is not worth living."[102] He's not wrong. I've discovered that an intentional prayer life can help shape a good and godly day, and when you rinse and repeat, it produces a life worth living that dramatically reduces regrets and the need for do-overs.

Strategy and Tactics

Reading through the Gospels, we know Jesus spent much time praying. He spent forty days fasting and praying before he began his ministry.[103] Long days of teaching and healing others were often followed by lonely hours of prayer and reflection. As witnesses to his prayer life, the disciples asked Jesus to teach them how to pray. He taught them what we know as "The Lord's Prayer."[104] As I have studied and used this prayer, I've come to appreciate it for its strategy, tactics, and simplicity. Strategy matters. Strategy requires stepping back, identifying your main objective, creating a plan that includes multiple minor tactics, and praying through those tactics.

---

102 "The unexamined life is not worth living," Wikipedia, last edits February 13, 2024, https://en.wikipedia.org/wiki/The_unexamined_life_is_not _worth_living.

103 Luke 4:2; Matthew 4:2

104 Luke 11:1; Matthew 6:9–13

Others have told me they found it helpful when I shared my strategy and tactics in prayer. I hope the ideas will help you, but don't do what I do; do what feeds your soul. Don't be afraid to engage your imagination and experiment. Baby steps are the best way to start a new endeavor. My process has evolved because I'm not the same person I was twenty years ago … hopefully. Tom Morris, author and motivational speaker, said, "You are either getting better or getting worse, but you are never staying the same."[105] That certainly describes my prayer experience.

Strategy

The first part of my two-part strategy is to press into the two greatest commandments: love God and love others. I typically have seven categories of prayer emphasis each year. Seven, in the Bible, often symbolizes completeness and perfection. I use a hub-and-spoke prayer strategy with the Father, Son, and Holy Spirit in the center (hub), connecting to the other areas of intentionality and focus (spokes). Since the first strategy's focus is love, logically, the spokes are relationship-driven: spouse, family, work family, extended family, spiritual family, and other vital relationships.

Since the late 1990s, typically in the last week of December, I prayerfully examine the previous twelve months, consider where Jesus is leading in the New Year, and document the results in my journal. The process includes a meaningful investment of time for reflection and writing to record how we have seen God at work in and around us. It is a critical step because it generates overwhelming joy, gratitude, and awe, overflowing with praise to God. Who

---

105 Tom Morris, "In this life, we're either getting better or we're getting worse …," Heroic.us, accessed July 25, 2024, https://www.heroic.us/quotes/tom-morris/in-this-life-were-either-getting-better-or-were-getting.

can remember what we were thinking about our lives when 2010 turned into 2011? One of the blessings of this habit is that I can give you five pages of the needs we were praying about then and how we saw God work in and around us because I just reread them. Ditto for every year since.

I also record a list of prayers, hopes, and dreams for the following year. These aren't goals, and this is not goal-setting. This is prayerful reflection and examination combined with necessary course corrections and dreams for the coming year. This differs from goal-setting because we co-labor with God, joining him in his actions. Zig Ziglar said, "If you aim at nothing, you will hit it every time."[106] We are asking God, "What can we aim at together?" The aim is to get on his agenda, not to get him on ours. We want his will and best because it is always better than ours. Always! This is the power of reflection and intentionality. And by now, I hope you can imagine this is much more than traditional church activities.

When I stop looking forward to my annual reflection time, it is a sign that my strategy has gotten stale. If I'm bored, so is God. That's when I tinker with the process until it gets fun again.

The second part of our strategy is pressing into Romans 16:20, "The God of peace will soon crush Satan under your feet." The enemy and his followers are organized, strategic, and tactical in their approach. They have control of most of the government, media, entertainment industry, and primary and higher education institutions. Their influence is undeniable, and we live in a time when good is now called evil and evil things are called good. This

---

106 Zig Ziglar according to Quotable Quotes, "If you aim at nothing, you will hit it every time," Goodreads.com, accessed July 25, 2024, https://www.goodreads.com/quotes/78121-if-you-aim-at-nothing-you-will-hit-it-every.

absurdity knows no limit; our leaders aren't able to define what a woman is![107]

Prayer is the foundation of living a victorious and abundant life. It was true for Jesus; logically, it is especially critical for us. His followers are not promised an easy life, but the opposite. Jesus said we would have trouble in this world: "If the world hates you, keep in mind that it hated me first."[108] The good news for those in Christ is that the battle has been won. We are on the winning team. Evil, sin, and death have been defeated but have not been vanquished … yet. Work remains to be done, and that's where prayer plays an important role.

In Ephesians, the Apostle Paul wrote that our struggle is not against flesh and blood but against powers and principalities of this dark world and spiritual forces of evil in the heavenly realms. He encourages us to put on the whole armor of God so that we can battle the devil's schemes. He admonishes us to pray, "And pray in the Spirit on all occasions with all kinds of prayers and requests. With this in mind, be alert and always keep on praying for all the Lord's people."[109] Sharon and I have identified several counterfeit cultural narratives where we storm the gates of hell in the name of Jesus to erase them from the planet. When you prayerfully examine all that is wrong in our country and peel back the layers, you will uncover the origins of these lies. We have incorporated into our strategy those powers, principalities, and spiritual forces of evil responsible for perpetuating these crippling narratives.

107 Alia E. Dastagir, "Marsha Blackburn asked Ketanji Brown Jackson to define 'woman.' Science says there's no simple answer," USA Today, updated March 27, 2022, https://www.usatoday.com/story/life/health-wellness/2022/03/24/marsha-blackburn-asked-ketanji-jackson-define-woman-science/7152439001/.
108 John 15:18
109 Ephesians 6:10–19

The battle for the hearts and souls of those we love begins on our knees. We change the world one heart at a time.

Daily Tactics

On most days, Sharon and I pray together as we walk through our neighborhood. Every day of the week has a different prayer emphasis based on the hub-and-spokes love strategy (spouse, family, work family, extended family, spiritual family, and other vital relationships):

> Every day – We pray for our Extended family. These are the folks I imagine around our deathbeds—our inner circle.

> Sunday – We pray for everyone in our Spiritual/ church family by name and eventually memorize them. If that's impossible, find something that makes sense in your context. It's helped us get to know their children.

> Monday – We pray for Missionaries and Ministries we support financially and those our church supports. These are now some of our most treasured relationships.

> Tuesday – We pray for individuals and people groups undergoing great Trials. A trial can be an illness, the death of a loved one, war, famine, flood ... whatever God puts on your heart.

Wednesday – We pray for **W**ork families, our colleagues, and their families. This list has grown over the years, but I've still managed to memorize them and all of their children and some grandchildren. You can show God's love to others when you ask about their spouse, children, or grandchildren by name. It's simple but powerful.

Thursday – We pray for our **T**own, our neighbors, city officials, and other organizations we support in our city. It's foundational to loving and getting to know your neighbors.

Friday – We pray for everyone in our birth **F**amilies, nieces, nephews, and great-nieces and nephews. This changes as family members die, marry, and new babies arrive. We imagine everyone at the wedding supper of the Lamb. We want everyone to be there!

Saturday – This day is open, and we pray for anything and anyone in our hearts that day with **S**pecial needs. There is always **S**omething or **S**omeone who can use more prayer support.

The Lord's Prayer Unpacked

When Sharon and I pray, we use the Lord's Prayer as our guide. Each morning, we pray through it twice. The first time we pray, it is exactly as we learned it. The second time through, we use it as an outline but go deeper and unpack layers of meaning gleaned from the scriptures. It's hard for me to imagine that with all the time Jesus spent in prayer, he recited the same prayer repeatedly. Our prayers are more conversational and personal. Everyone we pray for that day comes under the umbrella of this prayer, and we sprinkle any specific needs as we feel led.

- "Our Father, who art in heaven, hallowed be Thy Name." When the disciples asked Jesus to teach them to pray, he began with "Our Father," which is also how we start each day. We know our priority is our relationship with the One True God. Jesus prayed that we would know him and the Father.[110] He said loving God was the greatest commandment.[111] We acknowledge and thank him for our adoption into his forever family; he is our "Abba, Father,"[112] and we can come boldly into his presence knowing we are more loved and accepted than we ever dared to hope. I like to call him Papa God.

- "Thy Kingdom come, Thy Will be done on earth as it is in heaven." This was the next thing Jesus told them to pray. He also said, "I tell you that if two of you on earth agree about anything you ask for, it will be done for them by my Father in heaven. For where two or three gather in my name, there am I with them."[113] When we pray this, we imagine that we are coming into agreement not only with each other but with Jesus. It was his idea, and he prayed it first. We ask ourselves, *What is it about heaven we want on earth?* There is no sin, evil, disease, or death in heaven. We want less of that and more of the best of heaven: beauty, goodness, and

---

110 John 17:20–21
111 Matthew 22:37–38
112 Romans 8:15
113 Matthew 18:19–20

truth. We want him to rule and reign in our hearts and our city. Most of all, we want more of him! Some days, we pray for the Lord's imminent return.

- "Give us this day our daily bread." This is the grace we will need for the day. We give thanks and acknowledge our complete dependence on him for our provision. Daily bread has a different focus for many who don't know where their next meal comes from. Even though that is not our current reality, we know all that we are and have come from him.

- "Forgive us our debts as we forgive our debtors." We have memorized Psalm 51 and pray bits and pieces of David's prayer of repentance after Nathan confronted him about committing adultery with Bathsheba. His language and imagery capture our broken condition and failures and God's ability to cleanse and restore us. He prayed, "My sacrifice, O God, is a broken spirit; a broken and contrite heart you, God, will not despise" (verse 17). I love the image in verse 7, "Wash me, and I will be whiter than snow." We are requesting this for ourselves, our debtors, and all the others who are the focus of our prayers on that day. As we do this, we put off the old self, as the Apostle Paul taught.[114] Holding this image in mind, we then put on the Lord and the whole armor of God.[115] We feel free to use our God-given imagination as we get "dressed" for the day. Each article of clothing or armor has a specific purpose and is infused with his power.

114 Ephesians 4:22–24
115 Romans 13:14; Ephesians 4:22–24; 6:10–19

- "Lead us not into temptation but deliver us from evil." The last bit of armor is the sword of the Spirit, which is the Word of God. In Matthew 16:24 (NIV), Jesus said, "Whoever wants to be my disciple must deny themselves and take up their cross and follow me." We imagine we are reporting to Jesus afresh and ready to follow him into the new day. He came to destroy the works of the devil,[116] so we ask him to lead us not into temptation but to give us victory over evil in our flesh and the world. We go beyond asking for protection from evil and invite him to crush the adversary, his followers, and their schemes under our feet.[117] We execute an offensive tactic and name the demonic powers at war with the enemy of our souls and crush them in the name of Jesus, the name above all names.

- "For Thine is the kingdom, and the power, and the glory forever." We recently added the benediction prayer of Hebrews 13:20–21 to close our prayer time: "May the God of peace, who through the blood of the eternal covenant brought back from the dead our Lord Jesus, that great Shepherd of the sheep, equip you with everything good for doing his will, and may he work in us what is pleasing to him, through Jesus Christ, to whom be glory for ever and ever. Amen." It's a beautiful "Yes and amen."

Prayer Tips

- In the miracle of feeding the five thousand, when the apostles came to Jesus to make the problem disappear, he said

---

116 1 John 3:8; Hebrews 2:14
117 Romans 16:20

remarkable words: "You give them something to eat."[118] Jesus wants to partner with us in all things, especially in helping to fix our broken world. We spend less time telling God about a problem he is more aware of than we are and then telling him what should be done about it. We're prayerfully increasing the use of our authority as children of God to address the problems we and others face.

- I discovered a couple of tricks to overcome "monkey brain." (Monkey brain is a phrase that describes chaotic thoughts and emotions. Picture noisy monkeys swinging and jumping around, vying for your attention.) During your quiet time, try writing in a journal. The monkeys can't get in while we put our thoughts down on paper. When in the presence of others praying aloud, add your verbal agreement by saying "Yes" or "Amen" aloud, and you will be amazed at how it helps keep you connected to what's being prayed. Works every time. It will also encourage the person praying aloud because they feel connected to others.

- If you have never prayed aloud in the presence of others, make it a point to do so. And then keep doing it. God loves it, and the enemy hates it.

Pulling Back the Veil

During our Friday men's small-group Bible study, one of the more remarkable prayer experiences happened at Café 6100 on October 21, 2016. Lans Slack brought John Bell, a missionary friend, into town for a brief visit. Kevin Bowyer, Rick Herberg, and I were also present. Prayer was always a part of our study and fellowship time,

118 Matthew 14:13–21; Mark 6:31–44; Luke 9:12–17; John 6:1–14

but this day, I felt led to have us pray for John Bell, surrounding him and laying our hands on him as we prayed. The restaurant was empty; besides us, I recall seeing someone at the cash register picking up and paying for a to-go order. In my journal that night, I wrote: "It wasn't a long prayer ... and soon I heard a sound all around us. It was musical, humming or chanting with a Middle Eastern or Indian feel. It was beautiful and like nothing I've ever heard before. As soon as we stopped praying, the singing or chanting stopped." My journal entry was spot on; it was otherworldly, and I'd never heard anything like it before or since.

After we prayed, I opened my eyes and looked around. As I was doing so, Lans asked, "Did anyone else hear the music?" Kevin and I also heard it, but John and Rick did not. When I left the restaurant and was in my office, I called Dee, the proprietor, and asked her if she had heard the sound or if anyone had been playing music. She said "no" to both. So what was it?

Sometimes, the Lord will let us see and hear things from the unseen world. We heard angelic beings praying with us for John and his family. My friend and former pastor Steve Cathcart called this "God pulling back the veil or curtain between temporal and eternal realities, revealing a glimpse of things that are and not yet." It's on my list to look into when living on the other side of the curtain.

Another time the Lord pulled back the veil was in the middle of the night on Saturday, June 9, 2018. Sharon and I left home on Friday to drive to Buffalo to help care for my mom. She was at home under hospice care and couldn't be left alone. We left that morning, believing we would relieve my brother Alan, who had been staying with her. My dad had died four years earlier, and she relied on my brother Dave for many things, and we were all trying to pitch in to help. We stopped outside Pittsburgh to spend the night after receiving a phone call that Mom was being moved from hospice at home to a hospice facility. The nurse told my brothers that it was time for us to stop being her caregivers and focus on being her sons.

Sleeping was difficult, and around 4 a.m., I was lying awake praying when I became aware of what seemed to be my mother's presence. She asked if I wanted her to wait for me to get to Buffalo. She knew I was coming and would wait for me if it was important. I certainly wanted a chance to say goodbye, but not as much as I wanted her suffering to end. I told her not to wait. At 4:30, my cell phone rang. My brother Dave called to say Mom had just died. I said, "I know."

He Gets Us

Maybe you've seen the "He gets us" commercials about Jesus. I first noticed them during the Super Bowl. I'd like to see a series of commercial spots with "He's FOR us!"

When I first started following Jesus, my prayers resembled someone who was trying to convince a rich, miserly, tight-fisted God to open his hand and bless me. God reveals his excellent character and incomprehensible love for us through the scriptures and our circumstances. One of my favorite scripture verses that captures this is Romans 8:31–32, "If God is for us, who can be against us? He who did not spare his own Son, but gave him up for us all—how will he not also, along with him, graciously give us all things?" If God is FOR us ...

John Piper preached a sermon on this passage.[119] He wanted us to see this as an argument from the greater to the lesser. Piper

119 John Piper, "Who Can Be Against Us?" desiringGod.org, February 12, 2015, https://www.desiringgod.org/labs/who-can-be-against-us.

reminded us that the God who is forever "for" us has already done the one thing that would have been the greatest challenge for him ... letting his beloved Son be brutally beaten, crucified, and murdered. What could be more difficult? Nothing comes close! So, Piper asks, why would he withhold any good thing from us now or in the future? The Bible also says that while we were his enemies, Jesus died FOR you and me.[120] Let that sink in.

These powerful truths inspire and encourage us to approach the Father and pray strategically, tactically, and boldly. He's not a rich, miserly, tight-fisted God from whom we have to wrestle our needs and blessings.

He gets us. He's for us.

---

120 Romans 5:8

FINDING OUR PLACE
IN THE STORY

1. "If I'm bored, so is God." Prayer can get stale, but it doesn't have to stay that way. What can you do to help make prayer more engaging for you and God?

2. Socrates said, "The unexamined life is not worth living."[121] What might an annual reflection practice look like for you?

3. What did you find helpful, and what might you use as part of your prayer life?

4. He gets us. He's for us. How will this help you when you pray?

5. Don't be afraid to engage your God-given imagination and try new things in prayer that might seem unconventional. What comes to mind? Make a few notes now before you forget.

---

[121] "The unexamined life is not worth living," Wikipedia, last edits February 13, 2024, https://en.wikipedia.org/wiki/The_unexamined_life_is_not_worth_living.

26

The Lost Gospel of Jettekiah

"For everything that was written in the past was written to teach
us, so that through endurance taught in the Scriptures and
the encouragement they provide we might have hope."

Romans 15:4

Every Friday morning, for many years, I met with a group of men younger than me over breakfast to talk about life issues through the lens of scripture. I led similar groups, but this one grew from my relationship with Lans Slack. Lans and I had been meeting one-on-one for a while when we decided our conversations could interest others. I encouraged him to invite a few friends, and our Friday breakfast group was born.

We wanted to create a space where guys could feel safe and be vulnerable. This was not Sunday School, and we tried to avoid the typical "Churchianity" pitfalls. (Churchianity is watered down institutional religion.) With this group, you could leave your Sunday mask at the door. We met at Café 6100, and the proprietors, Steve and Dee, were excellent hosts. You might not think we were studying the Bible if you witnessed one of our gatherings on Friday. At times, we laughed so hard and got so loud it looked more like a party. I promise, we only had coffee. As time passed, guys came and went for all sorts of reasons. Some stuck around long enough and were given nicknames, like Lance Eubanks, aka "carwash." I loved Fridays and loved these men.

On many a Friday, you might hear me say, "That's not in the Bible, but it should be." The guys heard it so often that they decided to refer to these nuggets as "The Book of Jettekiah." Lans even presented me with a leather-bound journal with "Jettekiah" embossed on the front. Most of these proverbs are wisdom gleaned from my mistakes or pearls learned at the feet of my mentors. I am eternally grateful for the men God put in my life who profoundly impacted me. In this chapter, I've cataloged some of my favorites and given credit to the sources I still remember. These aren't meant to be biblical, but sometimes they rhyme with scripture, which shouldn't be surprising since all the best wisdom has biblical roots.

Jettekiah Proverbs

Buy One Get One (BOGO). (MJ) I do the grocery shopping for us because I like food. Seniors get an extra 5 percent off on Wednesdays at the local Publix, and the new BOGOs come out. My favorite part is when the checkout person tells me how much I saved. To date, my personal savings record in one transaction is $65.03. Booyah! I've adapted and applied BOGO to leveraging one activity into two or more. My record is four for one. When we lived in Charlotte and had dogs, we would walk two to three miles most days, praying as we went. Add them up: personal exercise, dog exercise, prayer, and spending time as a couple. Four for one … BOGO booyah, baby. Life can get hectic, and our calendars can get crowded. Life BOGOs can ease stress and anxiety while spending time on the activities most important to us.

"It's mind over mattress." (MJ) The key ingredient to every exercise program or Bible study is to get up thirty minutes earlier than normal.

"An excuse is a skin of a reason stuffed with a lie." (MJ) My daughter hated this one growing up, but I've heard her use it on our grandson. Reasons and excuses are two different things. Good and bad reasons are legit. Excuses are not. If the reason you are late for an appointment is that you didn't leave early enough, don't use lousy traffic as an excuse.

"We are not in the outcome business; we are in the obedience business." (MJ) Followers of Jesus are far too focused on the outcomes they are invested in. Results are up to the Lord; our job is to obey him. This is their number-one source of anger and disappointment. It's harder to love others when our agendas are threatened, e.g., election outcomes. Let them go; this is not our home. Outcomes are God's job.

"We landscape our sin." (MJ) When returning from mission trips in the Majority World, there was always a period of reacclimation to our reality. For example, what's the difference between our sophisticated security systems and their brick walls with broken glass and barbed wire on top? Our way of dealing with this sin only looks better. They are both meant to keep people from stealing our stuff or hurting us. We are all dealing with the same brokenness.

"There are worse things than being alone." (MJ) It's important to marry the right person for the right reasons. We've witnessed many unhappy single people become miserable married people. The latter is much worse than the former.

"That's not in the Bible." (MJ) One advantage of reading the entire Bible repeatedly is knowing what's not in it. The Bible does not say, "God never gives you more than you can handle." Most of life is more than we can handle. We need God all day, every day.

"We are motivated by pleasing methods or pleasing results." (MJ) I discovered many years ago that people motivated by pleasing results had better lives than those who were slaves to pleasing methods. For example, a student is presented with the choice of watching TV (pleasing method) or studying for an exam to get an A (pleasing result). The choice is between a little fleeting pleasure now or deferring it by studying hard so they can experience the pleasure of good grades later. A life built around activities that produce pleasing results requires discipline and sacrifice, but by definition, it is the life we would rather have. I think most choose pleasing methods.

"You can't talk yourself out of problems you behave into."[122] (Stephen Covey) Building or rebuilding trust is a process. You can only behave your way out of some problems, which takes time.

"You don't get credit for solving a problem you helped to create." (Gil Kennedy) This is especially true when we give or receive poor customer service. Fixing the problem helps, but it feels like a withdrawal, not a deposit, for those on the receiving end. We make deposits (get credit) when we fix problems others create.

---

122 Stephen R. Covey, "Reducing Recidivism Through Behavioral Change," The 7 Habits on the Inside (PDF), accessed July 25, 2024, https://www.franklin covey.com/wp-content/uploads/2020/10/downloads_government_ss_7 habitsinside.pdf.

"You get what you inspect, not what you expect." (Gil Kennedy) I have created a follow-up system to track things I expect others to accomplish because they rarely do what they promise. This system has been perfected because people are constantly testing it.

"Disappointment is the child of unrealistic expectations."[123] (Ken Boa) This is a cousin to "You get what you inspect." The next time you feel disappointed, peek at your expectations and ask yourself if they are realistic.

"The world will define you by default; God's Word can only define us through discipline. Even a dead fish can float downstream."[124] (Ken Boa) Quit striving and start training. The path to Christian maturity is paved by discipline. You are a beloved child of God. Don't let the world tell you who you are.

"Not all business is good business." (Larry Carroll) When I began building a financial planning practice, I tried to follow this proverb. Looking at your phone's caller ID and not wanting to answer is a good sign you accepted some lousy business. Life is too short to work with unpleasant people.

"All you can take with you is that which you've given away."[125] (Peter Bailey, *It's a Wonderful Life*.) This saying was under Peter Bailey's picture in George's office. Jesus said we can lay up treasure

---

123 Ken Boa, "Pushing Against the Tyranny of the Urgent," Explorers Podcast, January 23, 2023.
124 Ken Boa, "Biblical Risk Taking: Leveraging the Temporal for Eternal Gain," 2019 Kingdom Advisors Conference breakout session, February 21, 2019, Orlando, FL.
125 *It's a Wonderful Life*, directed by Frank Capra (RKO Pictures, Paramount Pictures, Republic Pictures, 1947).

in heaven for ourselves when we give our time, talent, and treasure away now.

"God made me fast. And when I run, I feel his pleasure."[126] (Eric Liddell) *Chariots of Fire* is one of my favorite movies. Eric's story is a wonderful reminder of the hope of 1 Samuel 2:30, "Those who honor me I will honor." I have felt his pleasure and presence with every word of this manuscript. I hope you experience his pleasure daily as you follow him.

"Grace is not opposed to effort; it is opposed to earning."[127] (Dallas Willard) Earning is an attitude. Effort is an action. Practice spiritual disciplines. Grace does not just have to do with forgiveness of sins alone.

"Laughter is the sound of the soul dancing"[128] (Dominic Done) I like to laugh … a lot. It feels so good.

"Gistisms." When I worked at Aetna Life and Casualty's Raleigh Marketing Office, Jim Gist was our boss. Jim was from Sheffield, Alabama, and whimsically shared many pearls of wisdom with his staff—some involved pigs. On one occasion, we presented Jim with a list of our favorites and labeled them Gistisms. Here are a few I will never forget:

---

126 Eric Liddell according to *Chariots of Fire*, directed by Hugh Hudson (David Puttnam, 1981).
127 Dallas Willard, "Live Life to the Full," Dallas Willard Ministries, dwillard.org, April 14, 2001, https://dwillard.org/resources/articles/live-life-to-the-full.
128 Jarod Kintz, *This Book is Not for Sale* (publisher unknown, 2011).

Jim's Pig Proverbs:

"Pigs get fat, but hogs get slaughtered." This was his investing advice after a run-up in the stock market. He said, "It's okay to get a little piggish." Sometimes, it is good to take profits and let the market cool.

"You don't wrestle with a pig. The pig likes it, and you get dirty." Don't take the bait from those who lure others into verbal arguments and sparring matches. They like it and fill some unmet needs, but you feel awful.

"Putting lipstick on a pig." The genius of some advertisers who can make awful things look and sound good. This metaphor applies to the marketing of long-term care insurance and Medicare Advantage.

"A bacon and egg breakfast; the chicken was involved, but the pig was committed." An excellent analogy when attempting to discern our and others' level of involvement or commitment to a cause or project.

Other Gistisms:

"You can believe half of what people say and 100 percent of what they do." I use this one frequently. People with various motives often say things they don't mean. It's a twist on the adage, "Actions speak louder than words." It also rhymes with, "You can tell when he is lying; his lips are moving."

"The proof of the puddin' is in the eatin'." The value, quality, or truth must be judged based on direct experience with something or its results ... not the brochure.

"Don't let people pee on you and call it rain." I experience this whenever I receive a letter from a business with the opening sentence, "We're excited to announce ..." and what follows is harmful, such as a rate hike or an announcement of a new benefit that disguises a change that is negative. It's a reminder to see through the spin to get to the truth. It's okay to tell them, "That's not rain, that's pee!"

"When the spotlight is on you, you better be dancin'." There are times in life when you or your performance is getting attention. In those times, you want to be at your best. When Jim said this, I always pictured the dance contest scene in *It's a Wonderful Life*.[129] George and Mary danced as the gym floor moved. They ended up in the swimming pool but kept dancing because the spotlight was on them.

Jim meant this story for an office sales contest performance. He wanted us to do well because we competed with other offices like ours. As Christians, people are always watching us. Let your light shine ... dance!

"Dance with the one that brung ya." I saved this one for last. My date to the senior prom ditched me after we got to the dance. It was hurtful but not unexpected, and it was bad manners, at best. I think many marriages end in divorce because

---

129 *It's a Wonderful Life*, directed by Frank Capra (RKO Pictures, Paramount Pictures, Republic Pictures, 1947).

we stop "dancing with the one that brought us." It's tempting to think the grass is greener elsewhere.

During a sales campaign, Jim focused on only a few agents who were his best relationships. These few were loyal and reliable. Jim's office always exceeded their goal because he always "danced" with the ones that "brung" him.

27

It's Been a Wonderful Life

"Jesus told this simple story, but they had no idea what he was talking about. So he tried again. 'I'll be explicit, then. I am the Gate for the sheep. All those others are up to no good— sheep rustlers, every one of them. But the sheep didn't listen to them. I am the Gate. Anyone who goes through me will be cared for—will freely go in and out, and find pasture.

A thief is only there to steal and kill and destroy. I came so they can have real and eternal life, more and better life than they ever dreamed of."

JOHN 10:6–10 (MSG)

"Better than I deserve" is my favorite response to the "How are you doing?" question. I love to answer this way; it almost always opens a door for a follow-up conversation. Followers of Jesus know exactly what I mean, but those carried along by the prevailing cultural currents are puzzled. Either way, I love the conversation that ensues.

In John 10:10, Jesus promised that if we followed him, we would have a wonderful life ... real and eternal, more and better than we ever dreamed of. It is one of my life Bible verses. He has kept that promise. All the reflections in this book combine to provide evidence of a promise fulfilled beyond all our expectations and infinitely beyond what we deserved. It's been an adventure full of risk and reward, failure and success, suffering and joy, entwined with profound hope and purpose—a wonderful life.

As I was writing this book, I wanted readers to see their story in our story. The promise of an abundant life is for all of Jesus's followers—and anyone who wants to come to him. A better life doesn't mean a perfect or easy life, but one with purpose and meaning. In the famous Christmas movie, George Bailey's life didn't turn out like anything he had imagined. Ours didn't either. But by the movie's end, no one would argue that George didn't have a wonderful life.

There have been many surprising revelations in telling our story in book form. God surprised me in every chapter with ideas I had never considered. I often began writing each day believing I knew the story I was telling, but by the time I got to the end of a chapter, the story's direction was not what I had imagined. Perhaps the greatest surprise was the revelation of a plot thread that ran through my adult life ... leadership.

Leadership cannot adequately capture the nuance of the plot altogether. Other descriptors are pastor, elder-at-large, disciple, and coach. But the word that encompasses all the others is under-shepherd. I was created to be an undershepherd of the Good Shepherd ... reminiscent of his words to me one night many years ago in Dallas, "Feed my sheep."

In 1974, when I left home to work a summer job as a camp counselor for the Milwaukee Boys' Club, I can see now why I loved that experience so much. This was my first time working in a role that fit what I was made for. I imagined a Boys' Club professional career for myself then, but that wasn't possible. The reasons why aren't relevant, but I was crushed when I left that work in 1980. Through the years, I wondered if I had missed my calling because I missed working with those kids. The call included those kids, but it encompassed much more. The Boys' Club was my first experience as a leader and coach. Even at nineteen, I profoundly influenced young children, my peers, and my elders. It was exhilarating.

I will always remember what the camp director told us during our first counselor training. He said, "There are two kinds of people: lifters and leaners. Which one are you?" Somehow, I knew then that I was created to be a lifter. For fifty years, God honed my "lifting" and undershepherd skills while I worked in my career or leading professional associations, church, and para-church organizations. In every context, I am constantly looking to make things better. That's what lifters do. And God will use those skills in the future … including the next life.

In Matthew 25:14–30, the parable of the talents, one message the master in the story tells the two faithful servants is, "Well done, good and faithful servant! You have been faithful with a few things; I will put you in charge of many things. Come and share your master's happiness!" The master, Jesus, puts them in charge of more things. They don't retire to a life of leisure on a cloud; their reward is a greater responsibility in the next life. (By the way, the American version of retirement is not biblical. Others have written books about that, so I won't belabor the point. However, now that I put it out there, something inside you is telling you it's true. Sorry! You're welcome?)

If you've read this far into the book, I hope our stories have been helpful as you follow Jesus or are currently searching for someone worthy of your faith. I'm just a beggar telling other beggars where I found bread. God wants you to know what you were created for and why you are here. But how do you follow someone you can't see? Jesus told Thomas, "Because you have seen me, you have believed; blessed are those who have not seen and yet have believed."[130] Jesus confirms that he expects others to follow him without seeing and calls us "blessed." To quote the great philosopher Carl from *Caddyshack*, "So, I've got that going for me."[131]

Perhaps you've heard the "Jesus with skin on" story. It's about a child afraid to sleep alone on a dark, stormy night. She calls out to her mom, who tells her not to be afraid because Jesus is beside her. The child replies, "But Mom, I need Jesus with skin on right now!" Along the way, God puts people in our lives who become "Jesus with skin on them" for us. I have been blessed to have many people who served me in that way. Ken Schultz, whom I have briefly written about, was one of those for me. The Bible reminds us that iron sharpens iron, and Ken helped sharpen me spiritually. Ken died recently, and his death was a profound loss to me and countless others. In his last years, as he battled cancer, he demonstrated what it looks like to finish life well. Ken set the bar very, very high. I aim to finish well and am grateful for his example.

So many of the biblical characters could have finished their lives in better ways—including Noah, Moses, Saul, David, Solomon, and Samuel. They all stumbled spiritually toward the end of their lives. However, their failure didn't disqualify them from their reward, and I am encouraged by the Lord's patience and grace toward them. Finishing well is not easy, and it's certainly not for sissies.

I've come to the end of this book, but the final chapter of my life is yet to be written. Writing a book wasn't on any "bucket list," but it did seem to fit the definition of a good investment of time. The Lord continues to put leadership and undershepherd opportunities before me. At sixty-eight, I'm confident I am in the last innings ... to borrow a baseball analogy. I want my life to fit the narrative from the Apostle Paul's second letter to Timothy, "I

---

130 John 20:29
131 *Caddyshack*, directed by Harold Ramis (Warner Bros., Orion Pictures, 1980).

have fought the good fight, I have finished the race, I have kept the faith."[132] It was true for my friend Ken Schultz.

If I die before Sharon, remind her that my tombstone should read, "Here lies Mike Jette … he lived a wonderful life."

---

132 2 Timothy 4:7

FINDING OUR PLACE
IN THE STORY

1. "I'm better than I deserve," to the biblically unfamiliar, is hard to understand. What do we deserve? Why?

2. Lifter or leaner. Which one best describes you?

3. What is shaping your ideas surrounding retirement?

4. Do you know what you were made for? Can you identify the thread in your life or connect the dots?

5. What do you want on your tombstone?

Thank You

Enduring relationships have made our lives wonderful. Writing about our adventures with Jesus caused me to reflect on the entirety of my life, and I realized that this would be an excellent opportunity to express my appreciation for those relationships.

My dearest wife, Sharon, you have been an exceptional partner. I've often marveled at how effortless it is to share my life with you. Your love and support have been the pillars of my happiness. I am truly blessed to have you by my side.

Karon Dyer, thank you for sharing your twin sister with me. I love you and all your beautiful family. Heather, Holly, Lisa, and everyone ... our door is always open, and we'd love to see you. Thanks to Rex and Jeannie (and Judy) for sharing your "Sis" with me.

The Petersons, Steve, Kari, and Chase, thank you for keeping life interesting. I know I can count on you to keep me humble. We love you guys beyond words.

Carl, Alan, and Dave: A guy couldn't ask for three better older brothers. Each of you brings a unique joy and perspective to my life. I'm so grateful we are still able to stay connected. We are all blessed to have spouses we don't deserve. Laura, Sharon, and Catherine, you have been the sisters I never had. Carl and Laura, thank you for inviting me into your home when I needed one. You changed my life.

Uncle Mike is one of my favorite titles. I was around for the births of Christopher, Timothy, and Jennifer and for much of their youth, for which I am grateful. Tina, Jon, Caroline, and Caitlin, we've enjoyed watching you all grow up into the special people you have become. We look forward to celebrating more of the big events in your lives.

I want to thank Ed Dore, Barb Badding-Ocarz, and Paula Badding for treating our parents like their own. You guys are like family; your kindness to "Mr. and Mrs. Jette" was exceptional and greatly appreciated.

When our parents passed away, our cousins Toni and Vickie Ann Jette traveled from California to be with us each time. Thank you for your sacrifice, thoughtfulness, and kindness.

If you are lucky, you may have one "best friend" from your growing-up years. I was blessed to have two. Bob Badding, thank you for wanting to keep in touch. What a privilege to have grown up together during the "Wonder Years." Dean Sienko, thank you for adopting me into your Milwaukee family. It's been a joy to be a part of your and Mary Jean's journey. Thank you for being my best man.

Thank you from "Michael Jette" to my Swormville friends: Alayne, Lynette, Jane, Kathy, Jack, Bob, and Marjorie. (And all the Baddings, too.) He is so glad to know you and hang out occasionally.

Several friends from BNHS have continued to hold a special place in my heart through the years: John Plante, Jerry and Mary Jo

Sheldon, Bill (GP) and Lynn Steger, and Sue Voltz-Farrell. Thank you for being great friends to me in high school and beyond.

To my KFP brothers, Jay, Mike, and the Garys … thanks for the memories. I cherish them all, and I'm grateful we all survived. You are important to me.

Some of my fondest memories are those from my Milwaukee Boys' Club days. I will never forget Schadow, Sam, Jeannie, Doug, Phil, and Amy. The summer of 1978 was my best, and there is no close second.

Life isn't linear, at least not for me. I expected a logical progression in my employment journey, but it didn't work out that way. I worked with and met some incredible souls during my stops at Allstate, Northwestern National, Aetna, Time/Fortis, and Equity Brokerage. You are not forgotten. I thank God for Aetna and Time/ Fortis Insurance on the first of every month.

I have been blessed to work with Larry Carroll for the past twenty-four years. Larry, thank you for taking a chance on me and giving me an opportunity. You created a place where human flourishing became a reality—well done!

To my CFA colleagues and family. What a ride! Thank you for being such a vital part of my life. I love you all. (I'm still praying for you.) It was "unbelievable."

Ben, Janelle, Micah, Caleb, Abby, Marvens, and Marvel Ganson, you have been integral to our lives in ways we never could have imagined. We are so grateful to be on a mission together. Ben, thank you for taking such good care of our clients and little flock.

If you are a client, you should know that my arrangement with Jesus for the Financial Planning Practice was, "He brings them, and we help them." Every one of you was a gift from God. I hope you felt well-served, loved, and blessed because that was our aim. Thank you for the privilege of working with you.

The Lord has placed many volunteer opportunities on my path through the years. Serving alongside dozens of gifted and inspiring people at Carmel Presbyterian Church, The Outreach Foundation, Charlotte North Rotary, Society of Financial Service Professionals, Kingdom Advisors, Agape Christian Counseling, Mwandi Mission Hospital, and the South Carolina Christian Foundation was a privilege.

Our entire African experience is a source of profound gratitude and wonder. We fell in love with all our Zambian brothers and sisters. Elias and Andrew continue to be our prayer focus. Life is hard there. Rury, Fiona, Lucy, and Cora Waddell will always be close to our hearts, no matter where they are in the world.

God gave us hearts to love pastors and their families, and he brought some wonderful spiritual mentors into our lives for specific seasons. It's been a gift to know Steve and Margaret Cathcart, Steve Cobb, Jim and Becky Szeyller, Scott and Anne Hilborn, Doug and Abbey Vinez, John and Carol Sittema, and Ken and Kim Schultz. We're so grateful for you and your families. Thank you for investing in our spiritual growth.

I must thank Bob Goff, who doesn't know me or how much he has inspired me. Bob's class for authors made me believe I could write a book. Bob's Dream Big Coaching program has allowed me to go deeper with some fantastic men. Ben, Zach, Terrel, Micah, Scott,

Connor, and Paul … thank you for allowing me to be your coach. We never get through a session without at least one Bob Goff quote.

The Lost Gospel of Jettekiah wouldn't have been written without guys like Lans, Lance, Bob, Matthew, Kevin, Barry, Rick, Joshua, Frank, and many others. Thank you for your patience, friendship, and humor.

Which brings me to this book. This idea became a reality because of my guide, Katya Fishman, my editor and chief cheerleader, Jennifer Jas, the creativity of Rachel Valliere, my design guru, and Carly Catt, my proofreader. Thanks also to Phil Smart from World Renew, Alex Greenawalt from Pathways Community Center, Brandon Davis and Daniel Hicks from the National Christian Foundation for helping with promotion and working through the charitable intentions and details. Tom Dundorf, thank you for praying for this project and being so faithful in praying for my family and me. You are a treasure.

I want to thank the dearly departed who joined the great cloud of witnesses mentioned in the book of Hebrews. Where would we be without our parents, grandparents, and great-grandparents? We look forward to reunions with those we know well and some we never knew but who live in us through shared DNA. We appreciate the part you played in bringing us into this world. We stand on your shoulders and appreciate your contributions to our lives.

And finally, writing this book has brought me more joy than I ever would have believed possible, along with a few surprises. The best gift I received was God's unmistakable presence whenever I sat down and opened my laptop to tell our stories. His Spirit has inspired and guided me from start to finish. I didn't expect to feel his presence so profoundly; I received his constant abiding delight and peace. Sometimes, usually in the middle of the night, he would inspire me with ideas, changes, and corrections in a voice that was uniquely his. I pray this book is a pleasing thank-you letter to our Lord and Savior, Jesus. Lead on!

About the Author

Mike Jette has dedicated over forty years to a successful career in the financial services industry. His unwavering commitment to integrating faith and finances stems from a profound belief in the timeless wisdom of the Bible as the cornerstone of a fulfilling life. Mike's fervent dedication to guiding small group Bible studies and sparking meaningful discussions, as well as introducing others to the teachings of Jesus, is undeniably captivating. His recent decision to share his transformative stories through a book reflects his unyielding determination to uplift and inspire others. Through his unwavering dedication, Mike serves as a poignant reminder that our faith has the power to truly impact the world.

Mike and Sharon live and learn in Rock Hill, South Carolina. They continue to walk with Jesus in their community and in their work throughout the world, and they are continually amazed by the wonderful lives they've been given. They are praying for you, dear reader, and want you to remember to meet them at Starrybucks on the other side.

Made in the USA
Middletown, DE
10 September 2024